"...doing strange things with peacock feathers in a hot tub."

San Francisco Examiner

"The erotic dream of many women."

Betty Dodson
author, *Sex for One: The Joy of Selfloving*

"A welcome addition to help couples expand sexual pleasure."

Sexuality Today Newsletter

"One cannot help but find beauty and pleasure by sharing in the intimate experiences described."
— from the Foreword: Beverly Whipple, Ph.D., R.N.
coauthor, *The G Spot*

"Useful not only in sexuality counseling but also in general relationship counseling and therapy."

Robert H. Rencken, M.Ed., M.S.
"Counselor of the Year"
(American Mental Health Counselors Association)

"A great guide to sensuous grooming for those who have decided to avoid the AIDS virus by avoiding the exchange of body fluids."

John Money, Ph.D.
Professor of Medical Psychology and Pediatrics, Emeritus
Johns Hopkins University

"Will help many people reach another level of pleasure and happiness."

Stephen T. Chang, Ph.D., M.D.
author, *The Tao of Sexology*

ROMANTIC INTERLUDES

A Sensuous Lovers Guide

Kenneth Ray Stubbs, Ph.D.

with Louise-Andrée Saulnier

Illustrated by Kyle Spencer

Secret Garden
Larkspur, CA

Published by   Secret Garden Publishing
                    P.O. Box 67 - RIT
                    Larkspur CA 94939-0067

An earlier version, entitled *The Sensuous Lovers Guide: Adventures in Sensuality, Sexuality, and Intimacy,* was copyrighted © 1986 by Kenneth Ray Stubbs, Ph.D., and later copyrighted © 1988 under the current title.
Portions of this text appeared in the German language, copyrighted © 1984, 1985 by Kenneth Ray Stubbs, Ph.D.

Printed in the United States of America.

Cover Painting: Kyle Spencer
Cover Design: Richard Stodart
Author's Photograph: Jim Dennis

ISBN 0-939263-14-9

The author gratefully acknowledges the following sources for permission to quote from copyrighted material:

Maps of Consciousness by Ralph Metzner, © 1971 by Ralph Metzner, published by The Macmillan Publishing Company.

The Wellness Workbook, by Regina Sara Ryan and John W. Travis, M.D., © 1981. Used by permission of Ten Speed Press, P.O. Box 7123, Berkeley, CA 94707.

Slow Hand by Michael Clark, John Bettis, © 1980 Sweet Harmony Music, Warner-Tamerlane Publishing Corp., & Flying Dutchman Music. All rights reserved. Used by permission.

Dedicated to the
students,
faculty,
and staff of the
Institute for Advanced Study
of Human Sexuality

An Important Word About Health

Discussing health concerns with a sexual partner or potential sexual partner is essential in establishing trust in a relationship, whether it be for an evening or for a lifetime.

There is an increasing public health concern about microorganisms that could create illness when transmitted through physical contact. This is an especially important issue when exploring sexual expression with a new partner or with multiple partners.

Sexual health information is usually available through community health agencies. Each individual can evaluate risk possibilities and choose for himself or herself what is best.

The purpose of this book is to teach sexual partners to be more sensual lovers. It is intended to give neither up-to-date medical nor psychological therapy. Whenever there is concern about physical or emotional illness, a qualified professional or agency should be consulted.

The author, illustrator, and the publisher shall have neither liability nor responsibility to any person or entity with respect to any loss, damage, injury, or ailment caused or alleged to be caused directly or indirectly by the information or lack of information in this book.

CONTENTS

Foreword

by Beverly Whipple, Ph.D., R.N.,
coauthor of *The G Spot*

From earliest childhood most of us received the message "don't touch." In the past, touch, and especially sexual touch, was limited to the bedroom with the lights out and was for procreation only. It was certainly not for pleasure. Later, society acknowledged that sexual touch could be enjoyed as an end in itself.

Only now are certain segments of our society beginning to realize that nurturing and appreciation of the senses can be pleasurable also. These are methods of communication, ways to say "I care." They do not have to lead to further sexual involvement, although they may if the couple chooses.

Massage is one method of touch and sensory awareness that is becoming more and more socially acceptable. In *Romantic Interludes*, Kenneth Ray Stubbs has gone beyond this. He has provided a framework as well as permission to experience giving or receiving nurturing in ways that can be perceived as sensually erotic. Again, these experiences can be enjoyed as ends in themselves. They are not presented as an appetizer to the main course of intercourse leading to the goal of orgasm.

It is my belief that we miss many opportunities to enjoy warm, intimate relationships and experiences because there is the expectation that touching and nurturing, especially touching which could be considered erotic, will automatically lead to penis-vagina sex. This does not have to be the case, and Dr. Stubbs presents a detailed guidebook to adventures in sensuality, sexuality, and intimacy, the only goal of which is to relax and enjoy pleasure.

It is my opinion that our society has to begin to give more value to pleasure and less to pain. My recent research involves natural pleasurable methods to alleviate acute and chronic pain without blocking other sensations. I applaud others who are trying to bring more pleasure into this world.

Romantic Interludes can be read alone or with a partner. It provides valuable detailed suggestions of ways to enjoy nurturing and being nurtured. One cannot help but find beauty and pleasure by sharing in the intimate experiences described in this book.

Preface

Safer-sex information may or may not be directly relevant to you and your partner at this time. It is, however, crucial that all of us be better informed. Ignorance, misinformation, and irrational fear are never solutions in public health.

In the appendix there is a section devoted to safer-sex. Throughout the main portion of the book, some chapters offer specific health and hygiene recommendations. In other chapters where there may be more concern about transmission factors, a "§" references the safer-sex appendix.

In *Romantic Interludes*, most of the suggested activities are considered "no risk" or "very low risk." Trust, sensuality, and playfulness are the focus. Here are a wide array of sights, sounds, tastes, and touches to nurture, to delight, to pleasure—all in short, easy-to-read chapters. You will find champagne, whipped cream, mangoes, bathing, massage, fantasy games, and many more ingredients of which romance is made.

Introduction

• *For Whom?* •

This guide is for sensuous lovers who wish to be even more sensuous.

It is for lovers who wish to say "I love you" without words.

It is for strangers who wish to explore becoming lovers.

It is for longtime mates who wish to relight the fires.

• *What Is a Sensuous Lover?* •

Friction sex is the rubbing together of body parts. It can feel pleasurable. For many it is the predominant mode of sexual expression. Friction sex, however, lacks certain qualities: the sensual and the intimate. Sensuality is the appreciation of all the sensory modes: flavor, fragrance, hue, texture, timbre, contour, and more. A sensuous lover is willing to take the time. Intimacy is openness to our own feelings and to our partner's feelings. It is honesty, vulnerability, and trust. There is willingness to listen and to communicate. While one need not necessarily be romantically in love, there is always respect.

In contrast to the repetitious nature of friction sex, sensuous sex flows. One moment may be spontaneously playful, the next quietly reverent. There is lingering, allowing the next feeling and touch to unfold. In exploration, new joys are welcomed.

To be a sensuous lover, then, is to blend the sensual, the sexual, and the intimate.

• *A Guide* •

We are all capable of expressing these qualities. Unfortunately, we may never have learned how to create conditions that encourage sensuality and intimacy.

Rarely at puberty are we sent to a mentor to learn how to be a creative lover. In school there are no courses in Sensuous Lovemaking. And the backseat of a car is far from conducive to learning about a slow hand, an easy touch.

Through trial and error and sometimes fortunate

circumstances, we may begin to integrate the sensual, the sexual, and the intimate. The process and experiences are unique for each of us.

What follows in this book reflects my own particular development. The various techniques, exercises,

---

If something strikes your fancy, cuddle up to your partner and ask for a date.

---

and rituals are suggestions—a guide for rediscovering some paths not taken for a while. Some suggestions will be directions for paths never taken.

• *Following This Guide* •

Romantic Interludes is for both men and women. Some of the techniques are applicable only to a woman's body and some only to a man's body. Most are for every body. And while the language implies male-female couples, same-sex couples have found many of the techniques equally valuable.

I have found it is often women who speak of bringing the sensual and intimate qualities to sex. Thus, the feeling of sensuous lovemaking is suggested by quotes mainly from women. And to minimize the use of "his or her" and "she or he," sometimes the instructions use female gender pronouns only.

Romantic Interludes is written so that you can begin anywhere. Simply pick it up from the nightstand beside your bed and look at the Table of Contents for an adventure of interest. Or just flip to a page. If something strikes your fancy, cuddle up to your partner and ask for a date (five minutes from now or next week). For encouragement, you might read a few passages aloud.

Some of the activities will take preparation; a few may take practice. Others require an open mind. For some, you just kick back the bedsheets.

Remember to be open to receiving as well as giving. Pleasuring another is a flattering gift. But unless you are willing to allow your partner to conduct occasionally, after a while the concerts may lose their excitement.

Regardless of your role, the most important guideline is to have fun.

One friend said it this way: "Pretend like you are a five-year-old—there's nothing complicated or serious about it. You're just having fun, like playing in the bathtub with your friend and a rubber ducky."

1

The Inner Chamber

One woman declared: "Sometimes I get so tired of just being a sex object. Not that I don't enjoy sex, don't get me wrong, I love it. It's just that I get so tired."

Even with religious and parental ghosts lurking in the back of many of our minds, we still enjoy sex, as this woman expressed. Many of us even passionately desire sex. But what we do not desire is being manipulated or treated as objects.

∞ ∞ ∞

For over fifteen years in Europe and North America, I taught couples' seminars on how to pleasure a lover.

More important than the techniques is the approach, I soon discovered in the early courses. The attitude is crucial. One seminar participant summed it up: "Some lovers think that gentleness is passivity rather than strength."

A woman participant expressed what she really wants: "I'm not a rubber doll. What's best is maybe one or two hours of some nibbling on the ear, some caressing, slowly undressing each other, then more caressing..."

If this approach attracts you, explore the following adventures. I will be suggesting some very practical ways to be a sensuous lover. Try them and see what happens.

To simplify the writing, the instructions in this chapter are as if a man is pleasuring a woman. Substitute a different gender if you prefer.

•   *A Sensuous Bath*   •

If you want to make your lover feel like Cleopatra, give her a sensuous bath. It will be both soothing and relaxing. The exquisite feel of soap and water lubricating your bodies will be equally erotic for you, the giver.

(*Cross References:* To make this an even more unique experience, you can feed her exotic delights while she reclines in the bath. See the next adventure,

Passion Fruit. If you have a shower stall, see *Summer Rain* (#3).)

The basic necessities are a candle, a bathtub, warm water, soap (preferably liquid), at least three or four towels, and a water-pouring container (preferably not glass). It is equally important to rearrange anyone or anything that might become an interruption or obligation.

If you wish to be even more luxurious, include a bathing sponge, a bath pillow for your lover's head, bubble bath and fragrances in the bathwater, and music (perhaps from a portable cassette player). Also, when

---

What's best is maybe one or two hours of some nibbling on the ear, some caressing, slowly undressing each other...

---

preparing the bathroom, remember to remove all the everyday reminders such as toothbrushes and reading magazines.

Mood is very, very important. Create a sense of

ceremony even before the bathing. If it suits her fantasy, you could refer to your lover as "Cleopatra." Invite her to slip into a comfortable robe. Then put on some relaxing music and perhaps burn mild incense. When she returns, pour her favorite wine and seat her in a comfortable chair. If you have a fireplace, light it. (This will also be a cozy spot to cuddle up together after the bath.) Now draw the bathwater, light the candle, and make the other final preparations.

When all is ready, graciously lead your lover into the inner chamber.

To begin the bathing, sit on the tub rim near her feet. After applying the soap to your hands, lift one of her legs onto your thigh and begin lathering it. Let your intuition direct your strokes. In bathing, the specific pattern is not crucial as long as it feels good to the recipient.

As you stroke, feel the luscious sensations of your lover's flesh sliding between your hands. Remember to have fun. Getting her clean is *not* the objective here.

After swirling the soap suds around her leg, pour water from the container to rinse. Linger with the falling stream of water.

Continue the lathering, stroking, and water pouring on the other leg and then the arms.

A hint: If your lover is shorter than the bathtub, there is a tendency for her to slide down toward the foot end of the tub. All you need to do, while bathing her arms and chest, is to place your foot between her legs so that her pelvic floor rests against your ankle. The gentle pressure on her pelvis often feels comforting.

Let the moods evolve—without demands. If she goes to sleep, wonderful. If she becomes sexually aroused, wonderful. If she has tears of sadness or of joy, wonderful.

Now slip into the tub behind her, with your legs surrounding her buttocks—perhaps a tight but delicious snuggle in most tubs. Then begin bathing her back. Focus a little more on the tight muscles on the shoulders and along the spine, but not too heavily. This is still an erotic interlude rather than an athletic event.

Next gently embrace her in your arms and invite her to rest on your chest as you lean backward. In this position, lather her abdomen and chest.

Remaining behind her, complete the bathing by pouring water for several minutes on the areas that are reachable. Heavenly…

Gently embrace your lover again, lingering in the water until she is ready to be dried with towels.

2

Passion Fruit

Sexual passion.

Men have it. Women have it.

But sometimes we *don't* have it. Sometimes we do not feel erotic. There can be many reasons: stress at work, ill children at home, financial difficulties. The weather is too hot, too cold.

In my pleasuring seminars, I have found that when romance is new, the fires of passion burn brightly. After a few months or perhaps years, the sparks become far less frequent.

In the ups and downs of everyday life, how might we relight those fires?

The first guideline is to invite our partner rather

than to expect or to demand. The invitation might be a handwritten note with flowers delivered by the florist. In one seminar a woman sighed that she really likes "little innuendoes" throughout the day, as if it were leading up to a nice evening. That flirtation, that suggestion that something special might be happening tonight. "You know, those little hints," she said.

A second guideline is to focus on the sensual qualities. Another woman told me: "I like a nice, romantic setting. Candlelight, a glass of wine, and to move into things slowly. Not just jump right into bed. I like the sensuous undressing."

As with a campfire, roaring passion begins with delicate twigs—the subtle touches, tastes, smells, sights, and sounds.

The previous chapter described how to give a sensuous bath: seating Cleopatra in a warm bath, lathering her in soap suds, and pouring streams of water over her royal form. Antony is equally deserving.

To such a luxurious interlude for either a queen or a king, you can add passion fruit: champagne, whipped cream, and mangoes.

• *An Epicurean Bath* •

Your lover reclines nude in a bubble bath lit by a single candle. Waves of soothing music drift through the ether.

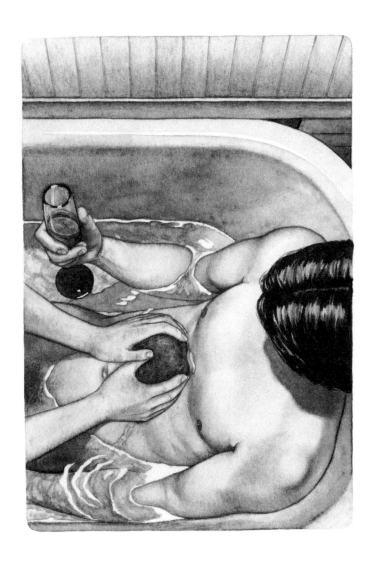

You, also nude, enter his bathing chamber quietly, carrying a platter of sliced kiwi and banana. Lengthwise sliced sections of mango ooze their sweet juices. Small clusters of green seedless grapes accent the redness of fresh strawberries and cherries. Shelled almonds are interspersed. A papaya, golden from the tropical sun, lies sliced in half. Filling its bellies are two white mounds of rich whipped cream.

Kneel beside your lover to ask if everything meets with his approval. When he says, "Yes," open the bottle of brut champagne. Lift a glass of still bubbling effervescence to his lips so that he might inhale its cold, rising mist even as he sips.

There are many variations on this theme that you can orchestrate yourself. Though, generally, it is best to feed before bathing.

The essential ingredient here is a willing recipient. You will also need a warm bath, champagne or a preferred nonalcoholic beverage, fruit (hopefully fresh), some nuts, and slightly sweetened whipped cream.

After a period of serving palatable pleasures, explore the following erotic tactile adventures.

For a *Palm Sundae*, place whipped cream and several fruits such as banana, mango, papaya, and strawberries in your palm. Make a sort of purée with the edge of a spoon. (You might invite your lover to close his eyes and listen to the sensuous sounds.) To feed, place the edge of your hand against his lips. Squeezing your fingers against your palm, slowly ooze the lusciousness through his lips. Ummmm...

Now apply whipped cream to his chest and abdomen—perhaps part of the *Palm Sundae* is already there. Delicately slide your palm over his glistening body.

A reminder: Sugar is very unhealthy inside the vagina. Be sure to rinse off all the whipped cream before intercourse.

Once the section of mango has been devoured, slide the inside surface of the mango peel across your

---

That suggestion that something special might be happening tonight...

---

lover's flesh. (Alternatives could be the inside surface of the papaya or the peeled persimmon flesh.) This is possibly the most erotic sensation on Earth!

With traces of cream and fruit lingering on his body, rinse with...yes, champagne from the glass. If he should scream, "Too extravagant," lavish even more effervescence upon him.

If you wish to partake directly in the pleasure,

apply the champagne with your lips and tongue. With the *Champagne Kiss,* allow the nectar to flow from your lips to his. For his neck, nipples, fingers, and toes, encircle your lips and tongue and suck, slide, and twirl as the bubbling coolness trickles down.

For the crowning experience, invite your lover to slowly stand—if he can. Then apply a generous portion of whipped cream to his chest and abdomen. Step into the tub and ask him to embrace you tightly. Remember, hold on!

From the bottle, pour champagne between your breasts and his chest. Let the cold, sparkling excitement slither down your abdomens and genitals. Be careful, though, not to swoon or lose your balance on the slippery bathtub surface.

After this *Champagne Shower,* you might give Antony his regal bath.

3

Summer Rain

Recently I was lecturing at a human sexuality conference. A woman in attendance described in detail how her lover had once pleasured her:

"It went on for hours and hours—actually for a whole weekend. He started off with champagne. Then he sucked my toes. He ate me all over, nibbled and sucked. I would be lying down on my front, and he would rub his whole body up and down my back. He had different kinds of oils…oh, it was just so wonderful. He was very erotic, very sensual."

A man like this, according to many women, is hard to find. One woman summed up her experience: "There has usually been a lack of gentleness, and thoughtful-

ness, and playfulness—all the things that make sex loving and fun."

All the things that make sex loving and fun. But in trying to be a "real man," men sometimes assume the role of conductor in the symphony of lovemaking. They may be busy checking logistics. Hoping for TSO—The Simultaneous Orgasm—they might even strive to numb their sensations by mentally reviewing the multiplication table.

For whatever reason, some men can forget to be playful.

But playfulness does not mean tickling a lover's ribs. It is not jumping up and down on the bed when the other wants to cuddle quietly.

The key to playfulness is being willing to try something new.

• *A Sensuous Shower* •

One afternoon my lover took me by the hand and initiated me into something wonderfully new. It is a special pleasure called the *Summer Rain Shower.*

For me, showers had always been a place to wake up in the morning. They were a place to clean up quickly before dashing out the door to an important appointment. Well, now I know that showering offers benefits beyond hygiene.

Here are some of the delightful treats my lover showed me in the shower stall:

First, make sure there is plenty of hot water. *This* shower will *not* be a quickie.

Second, a mild soap, perhaps subtly fragranced, is essential. Some liquid soaps have even more lather

---

With your lips, your fingertips, your whispers, describe to your lover the pleasures she or he brings you.

---

than solid ones. Other possible accessories might be a bathing sponge, a pouring pitcher (not of glass), and a loofah. A showerhead with variable intensities and a pulsing action is nice but by no means necessary.

Being in the right mood is important for this frolic. If your lover is feeling tense or tired, on the sofa try ten minutes of caressing strokes or serve a glass of wine with soothing music. When you are both ready, you might begin by slowly undressing each other.

Now comes the exquisite alchemy of soap, water, and body slithering against body.

With the water temperature at "enjoyable," apply the soap. Lavish it on your arms, chest, abdomen, and genitals. Feel your pleasure building.

Now use your entire torso to lather your lover. Never rush. Linger on each sensuous inch. Let your hands and body softly sculpture each curve. Explore each groove and ridge. Without words, let your fingers speak of love and beauty.

If the shower spray is rinsing away the soap, adjust the intensity and angle. And simply apply more soap.

One of my favorite positions is to stand behind my lover. My chest and pelvis can massage her back and buttocks while my hands stroke her belly. Sometimes I slide my embrace up and down her slippery body.

This position is also wonderful for sucking and nibbling your lover's neck. Especially enjoy the smooth textures beneath your lips.

(*Cross References:* For a variety of "sucking and nibbling" techniques, see *Lolita's Lips* (#8) and *The Big, Bad Wolf* (#9).)

Should passionate desire arise, there are two cautions: Do not slip and fall. And rinse all soap from the genitals since some ingredients could be very irritating inside the vagina.

In my first sensuous shower, my lover improvised a ceremonial chant. She was like an angel lullabying as we soared to the heavens.

Even if you do not have a trained voice, enfold your lover in your arms and hum softly. The melody might be your lover's favorite or one you originate spontaneously. If you are self-conscious about singing, remember that the soft roar of the spray and the echo of the shower chamber make all voices melodious.

To complete your sensuous interlude, rinse your lover with soothing streams of water from the sponge or pitcher. Then dry with soft towels. (To keep the mood, pat dry rather than slide the towel across the skin.)

After the shower, the two of you might snuggle under the covers or rest by the fire. With your lips, your fingertips, your whispers, describe to your lover the pleasures she or he brings you.

4

Hidden Treasures

"I certainly want a man to fondle my breasts and my genitals," exclaimed a woman in one of my seminars. Then she added, "but that's not all of me! I want to enjoy other parts of my body also. A good lover knows how to pleasure all of my body—and my mind."

∞ ∞ ∞

One day in school when I was thirteen, the teacher suddenly called on me to give a recitation.

Elocution from memory was scary enough. But even worse, at that very moment I happened to have a full erection.

If you are a man, perhaps you remember those

teen years—erections suddenly arising for no reason at all.

I was in puberty, and my penis was hard. Very hard, in fact. And I was wearing tight, black cotton pants. They had been washed and ironed with starch so often that the zipper flap shined.

In an embarrassing shuffle, I managed to get to the front of the room, turn, and face my peers. Then someone focused a spotlight on the silvery black bulge in my crotch—well, it felt as if there were a spotlight.

With experiences like this, it is very easy for men to be aware of their sex organs. And for many reasons,

---

And if you have peacock feathers, sensuous fabrics, or soft fur...

---

men often develop a fascination for women's sex organs. "Tits and Ass" is the street vernacular. "Come see Juicy Lucy," hawks the barker outside the live nude shows.

For eons, erect nipples and lubricated labia have been desired, craved, lusted after. Without such sexual attractions the species of Homo sapiens would not exist. This view, unfortunately, relegates sex to little more than a biological drive.

And as the woman who referred to her breasts and genitals exclaimed, "that's not all of me!"

What I hear from many liberated women is that they love sex—but sex that is caring, lingering, and playful.

A friend describes her preferred lovemaking this way: "I'm like an instrument being tuned. Each tuning, each song, is different. Sometimes my body is not in the mood. My lover and I might need to explore different chords. I really enjoy my whole body being strummed up and down."

Too often we assume that we know where and how our lover likes to be strummed, but our assumptions about another's pleasure zones are not always correct. To check them out, I recommend playing the following tune.

• *Pleasure Mapping* •

Your fingernails across your lover's shoulder, your hair down the buttocks, your tongue between toes, your palm resting gently on the abdomen: These can be very different experiences for your partner.

In pleasure mapping, you discover the highs and the lows. This is an exploration of various touches over your lover's entire body to find what and where turn on...or off.

In response to each touch, the recipient communicates by a number the degree of desirability or undesirability of each sensation. This is an indication of pleasure zones, not a measure of how well you are touching.

A response can range between "plus three" and "minus three." "Zero" is neutral. "Plus one" is "I like it." "Plus two" is "I really like it." And "plus three"..."Oh, my God!"

For minuses, a higher number means a more undesirable sensation.

Begin by inviting your lover to simply lie facedown, nude or minimally clothed. Then apply a series of uncomplicated touches. After each touch, the recipient will communicate a response number.

This could be the most exciting scientific research you'll ever try. Vary the direction of the touches: up, down, sideways. Vary the pressure from firm to light. Vary the type of touch, perhaps a caress, a squeeze, a tap, or remain still.

It is very important to limit the area your touch covers to not more than about five inches. Anything more might mix, for example, a "plus two" and a "zero" area.

In this research, there are two guidelines. First, pain is not the objective. If you should discover a minus response, avoid repeating that particular touch on that part of the body.

Second, do not seek "plus threes." For now, this is

exploration. Erotic caressing comes later.

Begin mapping the upper back, moving down to the feet. Once there, ask your partner to turn over. Now begin at the feet, coming up the legs, torso, arms, and finally the neck and head.

After about thirty minutes, you are likely to find that your lover is "turned on *all* over."

Once you have mapped the entire body, gracefully connect every part with long, flowing, erotic caresses. At this point, your lover no longer need respond with numbers.

And if you have peacock feathers, sensuous fabrics, or soft fur…ummmm.

5

Lingering in the Afterglow

To be a better lover, we could linger together a while after making love.

"Maybe cuddling or talking afterward," sighed one woman. "Or maybe showering together or caressing each other. It's wonderful when my husband doesn't end it all with his orgasm."

∞ ∞ ∞

During a visit to Italy, I heard an often told story. Michelangelo was questioned by an adversary as to why God had favored Michelangelo with a special talent for sculpturing forms into marble.

The artist replied that his talent did not have to do with sculpturing *into* stone. Rather, it was an ability to find the beauty God had already created in marble. He only smoothed away the rough edges so all could perceive God's creation.

If we wish to be a sensuous lover, we need only follow Michelangelo's philosophy.

•   *A Facial Massage*   •

The next time you want for your lover to radiate the beauty of a Madonna or a David, linger in the afterglow by sculpturing her or his face. (The following is written as if a woman is the recipient.)

Like Michelangelo, smooth away the rough edges of everyday tensions and stresses. Generally, try sliding the flat of your thumbs through grooves and along ridges to discover the beauty below. Let the sculpture's lines reveal themselves.

To begin, tell your lover you have a special treat and invite her to lie on her back. You will need to slowly disentangle your bodies from the last passion position. S-L-O-W-L-Y is the key word.

Softly caress or kiss her abdomen, breasts, and throat while sliding to a sitting position above her head. Offer words of appreciation to smooth her mind. Stimulate her olfactory sense by rubbing a drop or two of mildly fragranced cream, lotion, or oil into your hands.

When all is ready, begin the massage with ceremony. Simply rest your hands on her forehead in a "helmet" position: Your thumb pads are side by side on the middle of her forehead and your fingers are on her temples.

Perhaps close your eyes. Go inside yourself to find a quietness.

Without pressure, without strain, without rush, feel the temperature and contours beneath your hands. Place all of your awareness into your hands. Let them whisper, "I appreciate you," "I adore you," "I love you."

From this initial "helmet" position, begin your sculpturing on her brow. Use "T" movements, sliding

---

Like Michelangelo, smooth away the rough edges.

---

your thumbs up the center of her forehead and then separating them outward toward the temples.

Generally, the strokes start at the midline of the face and proceed outward. Your pressure can range from a delicate caress to a gentle firmness. When stroking downward toward her chin, always make the pressure lighter. If you are uncertain about the pressure, ask your partner.

Next come the eyebrows. Starting near the nose,

gently squeeze her eyebrows between each thumb and index finger. While continuing the squeeze, slide toward the temples. If your lover is not wearing hard contact lenses, gently slide over the eyelids. Should she be wearing soft contact lenses, make your touch even lighter.

Always move slowly enough to appreciate the art beneath your hands. Take the time to feel.

Stroke along the bone underneath the eyes, across the cheekbone, and so on, slowly following the sculpture lines down to her chin.

For the hollows of the temple and jaw, you can make circular movements with the flat parts of your fingers (not the tips). Here, rather than sliding across the skin, slide the facial skin over the muscles beneath.

But there is more to come in the afterglow. Do not forget the forgotten pleasure center—the ears.

Gently squeeze the earlobes and slide your fingers off while pulling outward. Continue this pattern around the entire edge of the ear as your lover sinks deeper into her pleasure.

For the final touch, slowly and gently slide your index or little fingers inside the openings of the ear canals. If your fingers are too large or fingernails too long, you can cup your palms around her ears.

Closing off external sounds brings your lover to the womblike world of her own breathing and heartbeat. For some, this can be a mystical experience. This stroke is called *Inner Peace*.

After a minute or more, very slowly remove your hands, slip down beside her, and quietly embrace. Relax. Linger. Feel each moment.

(*Cross References*: As you embrace after the massage, explore *Unison Breathing* as described in *Love/Sex/God* (#24).)

Whether your lover has had an orgasm or not, your personal gift of a journey into the afterglow is likely to be placed in the museum of fine memories.

6

Ritual and Reverence

What turns a woman on? There are as many answers as there are women and situations.

Speaking of a former lover, one woman expressed it like this: "Foreplay was nonexistent. The warmth and the caring, as far as touch and body contact, was not there to provide the stimulus, the excitation, that I needed."

On my seminar tours I hear many woman of different cultures, different ages, single or married, echoing similar experiences. Little is orated about the size of a man's penis, the thickness of his muscles, the speed of his tongue, or the color of his hair.

Most often, women remember the man's attitude.

It was not *what* he did but rather *how* he did it—the care, the attention, the willingness to be open to his feelings. This is when I see women's eyes roll back in reminiscence.

∞ ∞ ∞

I have a friend in England who special ordered several exceptionally large cotton towels. They were a rich burgundy with the thickest pile I have ever felt. On those frequently chilly Atlantic overcast evenings, while he is giving his lover a massage, the towels are warming in his nearby sauna. Immediately after completing the final strokes, he retrieves the toasty towels, which will transport the fortunate recipient to a Mediterranean beach in Greece.

A California friend, who does not have such lavish environs, has a different treat for "special friends." He chooses a fine wine and prepares a delicious

---

**He escorts her
to a soft armchair
and removes
her shoes.**

---

dinner. When his friend arrives, he escorts her to a soft armchair and removes her shoes. By candlelight and soft music, he slips her feet into a basin of warm water. Soon the fragrance of peppermint soap ascends and she hears the "slush-smack" of his fingers swirling suds around her ankles...

∞ ∞ ∞

The greatest barrier to experiencing pleasure is our mind.

Either as giver or receiver or both, to soar to heights of passion, we must transcend our everyday, logical, sequential, judgmental, mental processes.

How do we do this?

According to one woman, this is how: "What I want is ritual and reverence. Slowing everything down. Deliberately breathing, and touching, and going very slowly."

When we approach a lover with reverence for his or her mind and body, and when we bring the ambience of ritual to lovemaking, our lover will never have complaints about a lack of stimulus.

• *A Foot Bathing Ceremony* •

Like my friend in California, you might give your lover a foot bath the next time you wish to communicate ritual and reverence. Afterward it will likely become an elevated-evening memory.

Very little preparation is necessary to give a foot

bath. The essentials are a willing recipient, a basin (plastic holds heat longer than metal), soap (a liquid variety may be easier), warm or hot water, and at least three towels.

To enrich the atmosphere of ritual, soften the lighting. A candle or a fire in the fireplace can be especially nice. The music should be soothing, preferably without words, which might stimulate thinking. A chair or the floor can be used, but be sure there is ample cushioning. A pillow for the recipient's head and a light blanket might also be welcome.

Anticipate possible disturbances so that they can be minimized. Disconnect the phone. Make sure you will not be interrupted by children, relatives, or housemates. Equally important, when you speak, let your voice be soft and easy.

As with any pleasuring ritual, begin in ways that invite your lover to trust and surrender. Request either by word or gesture that you be allowed to remove your partner's shoes and other limiting garments.

First let the foot soak (or both feet, if there is space in the basin). Then remove the foot from the water and apply plenty of soap.

Almost any stroke you make with soap and water will be exquisite. Slowly circle the ankles. Firmly slide the heel of your hand down the arch. Let your finger pads explore the nooks and crannies on the top of the foot.

Your lover may be ummmming or drifting silently on a cloud. Let go of any expectations and words. Allow your partner to flow even deeper into inner pleasures.

Here's an exquisite treat. With ample soap and water, gently slither a finger up and down between the toes, one after the other.

After rinsing the foot, pat dry with a towel and snugly swaddle the foot. Continue the bathing ritual on the other foot, feeling in your own hands the pleasure of touch.

When you complete both feet, let your lover linger. Afterward, you might cuddle together and flower his or her face with gentle kisses.

7

Fantasy Island

"Right now, what I would like to be doing to you is…"

As a surprise, pick up the phone and call your lover. When she answers, tell her how much you love her. Tell her what you appreciate about her.

And then begin to suggest a scene of pleasure and passion. Take her imagination on an adventure far from her busy activities. With soft words and a sensuous tone, weave a verbal web:

You are alone on a tropical beach. Lying face down, your thighs and breasts sink into the Earth's open arms. Nearby, taking you deeper and deeper, the waves pound a primordial beat. Your back basks in the brilliant sun as ocean breezes cool the perspiration from your body.

Lying motionless, you feel droplets of lotion falling on your skin. Across your back glide another's hands, gentle and strong. Spreading the glow up your thighs, skillful palms rise with your buttocks and reach to your shoulders. You dare not look, for you wish to prolong the mystery. Again and again you silently ask, "Who is this magnificent stranger?"

Feeling your quivering body, he whispers, "Let go. Let go." And then he...

===

Making love in a field at night in the cool of the freshly plowed earth...

===

Fantasy is like champagne for the mind, adding effervescence to lovemaking.

Especially nice are a lover's words and sounds serving as the guide. Where such a "guided fantasy" goes depends only upon you and your partner's imagination. To help set the mood, you might follow these suggestions.

Mainly you need to have your partner's focused attention. When there is romance and passion, it is possible to have this attention even in urban subways.

However, when adventurous fondness is not present, the mind will be more open to guided images if the recipient is relaxed. Cuddling, massaging, or bathing together (refer to earlier chapters) are wonderful ways to relieve everyday tensions. Perhaps spend a weekend minivacation together alone at a country inn. With the environment and mood set, begin to unfold the verbal fantasy. For a desirable scenario, sometimes we can spontaneously dip into our imagination. If nothing appears, try the following sources.

Explore a nighttime dream. A California woman had this one: "I was making love in the water, hanging from the beams underneath our house at the beach. Our bodies were swaying as the waves came in. I actually woke up having an orgasm from that dream."

Verbalizing actual events from the past is another possibility. "One of my most memorable experiences was making love in a field at night in the cool of the freshly plowed earth," remembered the husband of the ocean-orgasm woman.

If you and your partner are willing, taboo topics contain powerful emotional energies that can boost sexual excitement. These topics are useful for guided fantasies, however, only if both partners find them desirable.

Of course, there are movies, plays, and operas. They are filled with heroines, heroes, and passion. When I was a child, Superman with his x-ray vision was one of my favorite comics heroes. It was not until the Superman movie that I realized *all* that he could see: Speaking to the fully clothed, lovely Lois Lane, he describes the color of her laced underwear. Just imagine what you might see.

Erotic literature has been with us for centuries. And in the last few years numerous books have appeared reporting individuals' fantasies in explicit detail! I have a friend who frequently reads to his wife both before and after dinner. They also go to bed earlier than anyone else I know.

If playing with guided fantasies excites you, perhaps add another element: Be risqué in public. Careful though—legal authorities might not have the same fantasies.

Near San Francisco almost eight years ago, I went to the Ali Baba Café. What is unique about this restaurant is that each table is surrounded by a different environment. The one that my lover and I selected felt like a castle tower. It was raised about three feet off the floor and had cushions rather than chairs. Most important, though, the waitress had to first open a swinging door to serve us.

This restaurant is known not only for its delicious food but also for its casual service. So we knew it might be twenty minutes before the waitress would return—but then it might be five minutes.

Quite spontaneously, with excited gleams in our

eyes, my lover and I began to verbalize fantasies. Soon our fingers were expressing on each other's body what our words were describing: My lover, who pretended she was from another planet, had a tongue very long and moist. Its muscles enabled it to twirl itself around parts of my body like a serpent… Would we get caught?

Now, eight years later, we still have an Ali Baba twinkle in our eyes when we talk about that swinging door.

8

Lolita's Lips

I decided to ask my lover if she would be in an experiment with me.

After learning sensual massage with my hands, I wondered, "Maybe *oral* massage? I bet that lips, teeth, and tongue could make some very unique and delicious strokes. Maybe some chocolate syrup, some whipped cream, ummmm..."

"Why not!" she replied. Thus began a memorable afternoon. Here are a few of our discoveries. (There'll be more in the next two chapters.)

• *Oral Massage, Part I* § •

It's nice to begin the interlude with a sensuous bath or shower. Soap, water, and slippery bodies can relax even the most hurried minds. The seeds of erotic moods also are lovingly nourished in water.

(Cross References: For bathing ceremonies, see *The Inner Chamber* (#1) and *Summer Rain* (#3).)

Then with the telephone unplugged and other possible interruptions managed, light a few candles. Music could add more ambience if the selections are without lyrics and dominating tempos.

Daisy Kisses

Saving the chocolate syrup and whipped cream for later, begin your oral massage with a bouquet of *Daisy Kisses.* As their name implies, these are delicate, cheery kisses. I recommend using a tiny bit of suction from your lips with each kiss.

Most importantly, plant the *Daisy Kisses* over *all* of your lover's body. In my seminars, participants often find their entire body to be one large erogenous zone. This includes the neck, the fingers and toes, the small of the back and the buttocks, behind the knees, the ears, even the temples.

The Ice Cream Lick

Next try the *Ice Cream Lick,* just like licking a cone

of your favorite flavor while your lover becomes creamy. Though this stroke may lift a recipient to the heights of pleasure, it serves a lubricating function as well. With each tasty lick, saliva is amply applied to the skin. (For health reasons, many medical authorities recommend not including oral-anal contact.)

The Lipstick

After lavishly lubricating an area such as the inner upper arm or lower back, try the *Lipstick*. For this stroke, moisten your lips thoroughly. Then gracefully slide them back and forth over the area as if lightly applying a soft lipstick. If possible, only your lips' delicate, membranous tissue touches, rather than a mustache or beard.

The Snake Tongue

Now slither over your lover with the *Snake Tongue*. Perhaps on the shoulders or the palms, rapidly flicker back and forth just the tip of your tongue.

Succulent Suction

Succulent Suction might follow. After making sure an area is extensively lubricated, place your lips entirely on your lover's skin. Next create a gentle suction in your mouth, enough that the skin is lifted slightly. Then, while continuing the suction and full lip contact, slide along a path of saliva. Gliding along the inner arm or the inner leg can be quite delightful.

The Lollipop

With the suction and sliding combination mastered, try the *Lollipop*. This special treat is for any appendage that fits neatly into your mouth. After making a finger or toe very juicy, slide your suction up and down the appendage. (It is very important to maintain a suction.) Now add the magic of a fantastic tongue, twirling it around desirously.

Remember to enjoy the sweet flavors as your lover melts.

Pleasurable Protuberance

For very small appendages such as a fingertip, the clitoris, a nipple, or an earlobe, the *Pleasurable Protuberance* is especially sensuous. Focus your lips around a selected protuberance. By creating a suction, suck the flesh into your mouth. Then, while maintaining a gentle suction, squeeze your lips and tongue together to push the protuberance outward. Continue the in-and-out movement without releasing the suction or contact. (If you are sucking on an ear, be very careful your lips do not produce sounds which may be painfully magnified so close to the ear canal.)

Motorboat

Before discovering and refining these oral massage

strokes, I had often wondered what a woman would do if her portable vibrator's batteries perished or if electricity became unavailable for a plug-in model. Well, the following oral massage stroke makes a lover a very portable and very lively living vibrator.

Because of the sound your lips produce, I call this stroke the *Motorboat*. Pucker your lips tightly together while forcing the outward breath through them. If done correctly, the lips will vibrate, and you will hear a loud, puttering sound. (As a word of medical caution, be careful not to blow air into the vagina. This might cause a dangerous air embolism, which is air reaching the blood vessels through the uterus.)

At first your motor may not sound very erotic. But sinking into an ocean of pleasure after actually feeling the vibration on the palms, nipples, clitoris, or underneath side of the head of the penis, the recipient may no longer hear the motor.

With such delightful toys and your lover's entire body as the playground, you may find that an afternoon of playtime is not nearly enough.

§ Please consult Appendix C.

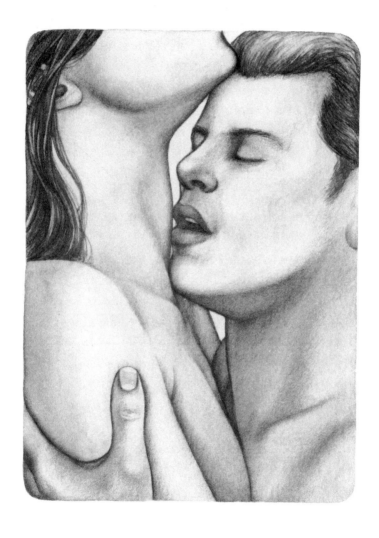

9

The Big, Bad Wolf

"What big eyes you have, Grandma."
"What a big mouth you have, Grandma."
"And what big teeth you have, Grandma."
"Yes, the better to eat you with," drooled the big, bad wolf.

•   *Oral Massage, Part II* [§]   •

In the tasty art of oral massage, masterful application of our teeth can take a lover into depths of pleasure unreachable perhaps by any other means.

Masterful is the key word here. One bite without sensitivity might be the *last* bite.

The Fairies' Dance

First, try the *Fairies' Dance*. Let the edges of your teeth delicately caress like tiny fairies dancing across a cloud. Here the touch is a slow, smooth slide across your lover's skin. As much as possible, allow only the teeth to touch: a mustache, beard, or nose contact might create a distracting sensation.

The Sun Kiss

A fine variation to accompany the *Fairies' Dance* is the *Sun Kiss*. While sliding your teeth across the many contours, exhale with a little more emphasis. Your breath's soothing warmth will be like the sun's glow at the beach.

Nibbles

Next try some loving *Nibbles*. While your hands gently squeeze an area, your teeth give one- or two-second nibbles. Each bite is large enough that both skin and the muscle beneath are included.

Especially nice for nibbling are the larger muscle sections. You can also include the throat, breasts, inner thighs, and genitals—but be *very* delicate.

The Slip and Slide

A similar stroke to the *Nibble* is the *Slip and Slide*. This oral delight requires a lavishly lubricated skin. Using your tongue, stroke and spread saliva until your partner is very juicy. (You might find the recipient requesting even more licking.) Now place your mouth as if to take a large nibble. Here, though, your teeth slide smoothly together across the skin. Be certain that they do not pinch the skin as they come together.

The Tiger Love Bite

Before moving to the more intense biting, a passionately heated body is a prerequisite! I suggest warming your lover's many grooves and delicious appendages with your moistened lips and tongue. (For detailed descriptions, you can return to the previous

---

Stroke and spread saliva until your partner is very juicy.

---

chapter for the *Ice Cream Lick*, *Snake Tongue*, *Succulent Suction*, and other oral joys.)

After these, your lover may be ready for the *Tiger Love Bite*. This stroke, however, must be applied with great care and sensitivity to keep him or her coming back for more. Depending on your lover's intensity of arousal, the same bite might elicit either anger or fierce, sexual passion.

Personally, I have found the *Tiger Love Bite* to be excessive for almost any place other than along the upper shoulder and back-of-the-neck muscles or the buttocks.

After you locate a spot where the muscle is thick and perhaps tight, you slowly sink your bite into the flesh. When you are first exploring such biting with your lover, slowly release the bite and verbally ask if the pressure was becoming undesirable. Such inquiries about satisfaction often indicate your care and the recipient is more likely to trust further erotic explorations.

After several intensity tests, slowly bite into your lover until you sense you are at the edge of pain—then bite a tiny bit more and release the pressure. If there is squirming and moaning with pleasure, you might hold the pressure for a couple of seconds before releasing. And if your lover would like more, continue succulent sucking and licking until you find another spot.

The *Tiger Love Bite* can also be exceptionally erotic in the heat of ardent intercourse. The combination of the *Tiger Love Bite* with coitus usually requires that the woman lie face down on the bed with the man lying face down on her back. Depending on the relative length of the woman's and man's bodies, other positions may need to be explored.

My recommendation is for you to wait until your lover is at a fervent pitch of desire. Then lovingly lick, nibble, and suck as high up the back and neck as you can reach. If your lover responds with more unrestrained movements, with more primitive sounds, gradually introduce the *Tiger Love Bite*.

Daisy Kisses

Sooner or later though, physical exhaustion overtakes even animalistic passion. This is a special time to soften the mood with tender *Daisy Kisses*—delicate, simple kisses like flower petals falling in slow motion.

Gentle Breezes

Follow this by blowing cooling *Gentle Breezes* through a small opening between your lips about six inches away from the skin…ouuuu.

∞ ∞ ∞

So the next time your lover calls you a big, bad wolf, you'll know it's *not* an invitation to read a bedtime story.

§ Please consult Appendix C.

10

The Garden of Unearthly Delights

• *Oral Massage, Part III* § •

The aphrodisiacal ritual that follows is only for the adventurous. When you are ready for two or three hours of playful abandonment, welcome to the *Garden of Unearthly Delights*.

Here are some of the preparations you will need.

First select a bedsheet that may never get thoroughly clean afterwards. It is also advisable, though not essential, to have a large sheet of plastic to protect the carpet, bed, or wherever the ritual will be held.

Since you probably will not have sufficient edible ingredients at home, you'll need to schedule a shopping trip. Unfortunately, fully ripened fruits may not be available at the market. So it would be best to purchase these a few days before the evening (or afternoon) of unearthly delights.

If by chance the scenario has not been deduced by now, here is what takes place in the Garden. A variety of fruits, nuts, and sauces are to be prepared, sliced, and then sculptured. Your lover's nude body, of course, will be the foundation upon which your sculpture rests. But this will be living, participatory art. You, in epicurean fashion, partake fully of your creation. Meanwhile, your lover, who just happens to be beneath your tongue, may well be entering the realm of rapture.

Depending on the season, here are a few fresh fruit suggestions.

The Goddess must have been defining the essence of pleasure when she created the mango. Golden in color with the sweetness of heavenly nectar and the texture of sexual satisfaction, this fruit delights both the palate of the feaster and the one feasted upon.

Other sumptuous choices would be papaya, bananas, strawberries, cherries, kiwi, seedless grapes, and maybe persimmons. One or two varieties of melons would make the Garden even juicier. Citrus fruits, for me at least, do not blend well with the following chocolate and cream sauces. But let your desire be your guide.

For the nuts, good possibilities are almonds, walnuts, and pecans. Some of these could be roasted but not heavily salted.

Remembering dietary considerations, a selection of sauces will make the feast even more luscious. Chocolate syrup is one. And if you have never tried real maple syrup, the darker grades are heavenly.

For many connoisseurs, slightly sweetened, hand-whipped whipped cream is a must. To make it almost orgasmic, purchase the thickest cream possible (but definitely without added thickening ingredients, which have somehow sneaked into some brands). Also, while

Golden in color with the sweetness of heavenly nectar and the texture of sexual satisfaction...

pressurized cans make for flamboyant sculpturing, I have found their whipped cream to be inferior at best and highly chemicalized at worst. But again, let your taste buds set the criteria.

For another special sauce, mix heated honey or maple syrup with sour cream or plain yogurt. Sweeten to the flavor that fits your tastes.

(Two notes about sugar: Be certain not to allow sugared ingredients into the vagina! They may upset the microbial balance. So shower thoroughly before any penetration. Also, too much sugar for some people leads to sugar highs, which then lead to sugar crashes. Have fun, but remember the parameters.)

There's one more selection: champagne. Most likely its fluid nature would not be contained well within the sculpture, but champagne is great for toasts at the celebration party after the gallery opening.

After all the selections are gathered, you'll need

about two hours of preparation before the actual ritual. Also, since you create your sculpture directly on your lover's skin, try to minimize chilled substances. Keep all fruits at room temperature and warm the sauces that are heatable.

As the appointed hour approaches, begin to fashion an erotic ambience. Make sure the room is warm. Unplug the phone, light candles, and select music. Do anything necessary to create a sense that there will be no interruptions.

When all is prepared, escort your beloved into the ceremonial chamber. After assisting with the disrobing, invite him or her to recline beside the beautifully prepared platters and bowls.

In a soft voice, ask your lover to let you know if any sensation or experience becomes undesirable. Otherwise, the only permissible vocal expressions will be moans and groans. Suggest taking a deep breath and allowing the eyes to close.

Then, turn the music up a little, cease verbal chatter, and enter the *Garden of Unearthly Delights*.

§ Please consult Appendix C.

11

A Slow Hand, An Easy Touch

I want a man with a slow hand
I want a lover with an easy touch
I want somebody who will spend some time
Not come and go in a heated rush
I want somebody who will understand...

Speaking for many women, the Pointer Sisters tell it like it is in their rendition of "Slow Hand."

Even more explicitly, another woman expressed it this way: "When a man is having sex with me, I love it when he takes time to find my clitoris and massage it and love it. Making love to my clitoris with his tongue, with his finger, with his nose, with whatever. I like it when he takes the time to make love with it rather than hurrying to find the spot and then attacking it."

• *Female Genital Massage, Part I* § •

One of those evenings (or mornings or afternoons) when you and your lover are not in a heated rush, you might try a slow-hand, easy-touch genital massage.

Before beginning, there are a few preparations. A massage oil will make some of the following strokes feel much better. Unfortunately, the "essential oils" and chemicals used to scent some oils may be irritating to the vaginal tissues. In general I recommend a natural, unfragranced, vegetable oil from a health food store.

The sweet thrill comes when the oil seeps between your relaxed fingers.

(Coconut oil is one of my favorites.) If your lover's vagina is sensitive to oil, an alternative is water-soluble lubricating jellies found in pharmacies. Since each body is different, it may take experimentation.

Don't forget the fingernails. They should be smooth and not very long. You might also want to wash your hands before beginning.

With the phone unplugged, soft music playing, the oil perhaps warmed, and whatever else that might set a romantic, erotic mood for your lover, begin by stroking her entire body. Try caressing places another woman suggested: "The tips of my ears, the nape of my neck, the crack at the top of my buttocks, the small of my back, between my tiniest toes. To be *totally* turned on, I need all of me aroused."

Sweet Thrills

As the mood becomes more desirous, begin massaging your lover's pubic and genital area with *Sweet Thrills*. Sitting or kneeling very closely to her right side, rest your left palm on her pubic mound. Then your right hand simply pours oil onto the back of your left hand. The sweet thrill comes when the oil seeps between your relaxed fingers onto her vulva.

Now with your hands alternating, spread the oil with an upward, sliding motion along the length of her vulva. (For health reasons, avoid including the anal area in this and the following strokes.)

Always remember to have a slow hand and an easy touch.

The Hair Tease

You might follow with the *Hair Tease*. Again alternating your hands, let your thumb and index finger delicately pull the pubic hairs.

The Voluptuous Vulva

For the *Voluptuous Vulva,* you give a series of strokes along the entirety of each outer lip and then each inner lip. With a thumb on one side of a lip and the index finger on the other, gently squeeze and slide off the edge of the lip. To maintain a continuous sensation, again alternate your hands in the stroking.

Even while you are learning these strokes, remain sensitive to your lover's feelings. She might be in ecstasy or in discomfort. If you are not certain, ask for feedback. A little modification of pressure or direction might make a major difference.

Ring Around the Rosy

Next, *Ring Around the Rosy* focuses both on and around the sensitive clitoral head, which is just beneath the hood where the upper parts of the inner labia merge. In the three phases of this stroke, I recommend massaging with the soft inner side of your middle finger.

First, gently slide up and down between the outer and inner labia on one side of the vulva and then the other.

There's no rush. So feel the especially luscious

combination of massage oil, vaginal juices, and membranous tissues.

Second, make a "ring around the rosy" by sliding your finger (and perhaps an adjoining finger) around the clitoral head in a circle in one direction several times and then in the other direction.

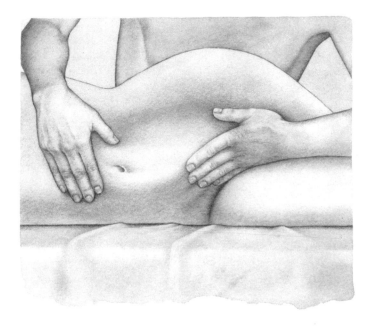

And third, pick "a pocket full of posies." Here you slide your finger very, very slowly up between the inner lips and up across the clitoral head.

If you slide slowly enough, sometimes when your finger reaches the underside of the clitoral head, genital muscles contract and slide the head down past your finger. "Ummmm," moans the receiver.

"Ummmm," moans the giver.

(There's even more coming in the next two erotic interludes.)

§ Please consult Appendix C.

12

Rockin' Around the Clock

Each woman and each interlude is different.

One friend describes how her lover once set a passionate mood: "First he stroked me with his hands, every inch of my body. Then with his mouth, kissing and sucking and licking. He played so long on my breasts and nipples, which are supersensitive, and on the back of my neck. But he never touched my genitals. Then he went down to my feet, my toes, and my inner thighs. He did that for well over an hour—until I was practically begging him to please touch my genitals. I couldn't stand it!

"At one point his hair accidentally touched them. Just that little caress made me rise up. And still he would not touch my genitals. He went back down my legs and back to my feet. And then his hands finally slid into my very wet vagina."

• *Female Genital Massage, Part II* [§] •

Rockin' Around the Clock

As with the fortunate woman above, when your lover is highly aroused after an hour of caressing, snuggling, and massaging, you might change the tempo with *Rockin' Around the Clock*.

Imagine a clock on your lover's vulva. High noon rests at the clitoral position. Six o'clock is near the anus. And the other hours fit accordingly around the clock. (In the previous chapter, you'll find some clitoral massage strokes to help wind up the clock.)

After making certain that your fingernails are smooth, short, and clean, sit or kneel on your lover's right (assuming you are right-handed). Along the length of her inner labia, slowly slide up and down with your right thumb's inner, soft side. With each downward stroke, your thumb gradually and lovingly enters her orifice. (Your left hand rests on her abdomen and the fingers of your right hand are on her pubic mound.)

It is very important that there be copious lubrication and that your touch is slow and easy.

Then, with your thumb fully inserted at the high noon hour, position it so that its soft pad is pressing upward on the underneath side of her pubic bone.

Just that little caress made me rise up.

Now rock—but not frantically as in the days of the Peppermint Twist. Instead, your torso sways your arm and hand smoothly back and forth about an inch. Here the focus is on creating a pressure contact from your thumb, not sliding it across the vaginal tissue.

After about fifteen seconds or longer, lighten your pressure, slip over to one o'clock, and rock again. And as you continue toward midnight, you will need to shift from your thumb to your index finger at about eight o'clock.

Learning this dance step can be a little complicated, but your lover may find that she likes the new beat.

Feelin' Good All Over

Before leaving the dance floor, I recommend a very sensuous slow dance that will leave her *Feelin' Good All Over*.

This series of strokes connects the pleasurable sensations of her genitals with the pleasurable sensations in several other parts of her body. Maybe you will want to use a massage oil—perhaps a natural, unfragranced vegetable oil, such as coconut oil from a health food store. An alternative is water-soluble lubricating jellies found in pharmacies.

Assuming you are sitting or kneeling on your lover's right, your right-hand fingers tenderly stroke up and down and around on her inner labia and clitoris. Remember, this is a slow dance.

Meanwhile, your left hand massages her abdomen. You can use a kneading movement like this: Slide your palm down the center of the abdominal muscles with your thumb and fingers on opposite sides. Then end each stroke by sliding (or gently squeezing) together your thumb and fingers.

Continuing with your right hand on the vulva, your left hand caringly strokes her right breast. On the nipple, your thumb and index finger lightly squeeze at the nipple's base and slide upward.

Now comes a combining of the wonderful pleasures of the genitals with the wonderful sensations of the neck and shoulders. With your left hand, knead the shoulder and neck muscles in the thumb-opposite-fingers fashion. Remember to be very light with your thumb on the throat area.

Now while your left thumb moves down to stroke

the inner labia and the clitoral area, your right hand can massage her inner right thigh.

After *Feelin' Good All Over* on her right side, gracefully move to her other side and follow a similar sequence, reversing the right- and left-hand instructions. In all of these areas, vary the rhythms and pressures. Be gentle. And never hurry.

After this slow dance, let your lover make the next selection. She might want to fast dance or she might want to cuddle up and go to sleep.

§ Please consult Appendix C.

13

The Gee! Stroke

Only a few years ago we rediscovered the clitoris.

When the popular word about this erogenous zone hit the bedroom, flashlights and mirrors were brought out to shed more light on the provocative subject. Vibrators and pulsating showerheads became common household appliances.

The clitoris became chic.

Unfortunately, like clothing styles and hit records, sexual expressions can become fashionable.

New information can deeply enrich our lives. But in simply narrowing our focus to what is popular, we often fail to listen to our own experience.

Fortunately, some women continued to pay atten-

tion to their own bodies. They said the clitoris is great—
but not the only answer.

• *The G Spot* [§] •

What was an underground murmur has now
emerged as the G spot. While it too has become fashionable, the G spot may be something you and your
lover find special when sharing close moments together.

Think of the G spot as a *sensation* rather than as a spot or location.

What is it?

Described as a location in a woman's pelvis, the
G spot is a source of pleasurable, sexual arousal when
it is stimulated.

Unfortunately, "spot" is not the best terminology.
It may be better to think of the G spot as a *sensation*
rather than as a spot or location.

Where is it?

Imagine a clock on your lover's vulva. Twelve
o'clock is on the upper portion near the clitoris.

The G spot is inside the vagina near twelve o'clock or perhaps eleven o'clock or one o'clock.

Its location inside the vagina is indicated differently in various books. It might be about an inch inside the vagina, just behind the pubic bone. Another suggested area is farther up inside the vagina, still near twelve o'clock.

Due to a wide variation in pelvic structures, the G spot might actually be anywhere from just above the pubic bone to somewhere near the uterus. In both my personal and teaching experiences, I have found that the most intense sensations are often in the area above the pubic bone.

What is more important, though, is that you and your lover try the possibilities and discover for yourselves what is the most pleasurable.

How to Discover the G Spot

Every woman does not have the same response to stimulation of this area. It can range from ecstatically pleasurable to neutral to painful.

If probing is too intense, pain can result. (Fingernails should be short and smooth.) When the G-spot area is first explored, feeling the need to urinate is a rather common experience. With longer and more gentle stimulation, the sensation however may turn pleasurable.

Many women describe this pleasurable sensation

as sexual. But unlike the clitoris, the G-spot sensation is often characterized as "deeper in the body," "inside the core."

Once a woman experiences and identifies a G-spot sensation, she usually locates it easily again. Unfortunately, the G spot may be hard to find initially. If there is a secret to discovery, it is this: high sexual arousal. The best time to begin the search is when the woman feels her desire building.

A woman can masturbate if she wants to make the first exploration by herself. With a partner, the addition of kisses, caresses, and whispered words may bring other arousals.

Often finger stimulation is more effective than penile stimulation. The best position is likely to be with the woman squatting or, if it is easier, sitting on a toilet. She can also try a reclined position on her back with her knees up.

If you are the partner, you can do the following. After gently introducing your index and middle fingers into her vagina along the twelve o'clock position, try two different movements. On a selected location, first slide the finger pads across the membranous tissue in a "come here" motion. The other possibility is to put enough pressure (not too much) to move the membranous tissue back and forth over the muscles, other tissues, and perhaps the pubic bone.

With either of these movements, a gentle pressure

from the other hand can be added on the lower abdomen just above the pubic bone. This may provide a better stroking surface for the inserted fingers.

Be gentle, be patient. If nothing interesting occurs after a while, be sensuous in other, more familiar ways. There will be another time to explore the G spot.[1]

The Gee! Stroke

This combines the best of two worlds: massaging the G spot and the clitoris at the same time.

(*Cross References: The Gee! Stroke* fits exquisitely into the strokes sequence of the previous two chapters: *A Slow Hand, An Easy Touch* (#11) and *Rockin' Around the Clock* (#12).)

Invite your lover to lie on her back with her knees up and feet on the bed or floor. Sitting at her right side, slowly slide your right-hand index and middle fingers to her G-spot area and begin the "come here" stroking.

At the same time, put a gentle pressure with the heel of your left hand on her lower abdomen above her pubic bone.

The final touch is a delicate stroking with your left-hand fingers on her clitoris.

You'll know where the stroke's name came from when she moans, "Gee!"

§ Please consult Appendix C.

[1] For an extensive description of the G spot, see *The G Spot and Other Recent Discoveries About Human Sexuality* by Alice Kahn Ladas, Beverly Whipple, and John D. Perry (New York: Holt, Rinehart and Winston, 1982).

14

The Hole in the Donut

A donut massage—that's what massage school taught me. The style was sensitive. The touches were soothing. The body was connected together with long, flowing strokes. Later, though, I realized that what massage schools teach is really a donut massage.

A donut, especially when tasted hot from the oven, is a sensuous pastry. But there is something missing. There is a hole in the middle.

Not a huge one, but nonetheless, a hole.

This chapter and the three before and after it are dedicated to teaching what you will never learn in a massage school. I call this set of strokes the *Hole-in-the-Donut Massage.*

• *Male Genital Massage, Part I* [§] •

"Hey! What about me?" men may have been wondering. The last three chapters have described how to give a woman an erotic genital massage.

Well, now it's men's turn to receive. If you are a man, just lie back and relax. The remainder is written to your lover. You can give feedback about what does or does not feel good, but don't try to instruct or massage her at the same time.

∞ ∞ ∞

It is best to start with flowing strokes to connect many different parts of your lover's body. Spread the oil, remembering that the more hair he has, the more oil he will need.

Suggest that he close his eyes and focus on your touch.

When you sense he has become more relaxed, try the following strokes. A few of them will be similar to the ones you may have already received.

The following instructions assume you are on his right side.

Sweet Thrills

Lift your lover's penis and scrotum so that your left palm cups the scrotum. Allow your fingers to be slightly separated. Now pour massage oil on the back of this hand. As the oil seeps between your fingers onto the penis and scrotum, he may feel a sweet thrill. Use plenty of oil, and with loving strokes, spread it thoroughly over all of his genital area.

The Juicer

This is sort of like squeezing your own orange juice with one of those old-fashioned, preelectric hand juicers.

Your left hand gently stretches the foreskin down along the shaft. Next your right-hand finger pads encircle the head of the penis and slide up and down along the length of the head while the fingers rotate back and forth. Vary the pressure and ask your lover what feels best.

What massage schools teach is really a donut massage.

The Snake

Like a sensuous serpent, you entwine the penis with your fingers and slither around just below its head.

Continue gently stretching the foreskin with your left hand as in the previous stroke. Facing downward toward his pelvis, your right thumb and index finger form a snug circle just below the head of the penis.

Rotate your right hand in a clockwise direction as far as your wrist permits.

Continuing the flow, lift your right thumb so your index finger can slide around until the thumb and index finger again form a circle around the penis.

If this sounds too complex, just let your hand slither.

The Countdown

In preparation for rocket takeoff, count "10, 9, 8, 7...blast off!"

Alternating your hands and using plenty of oil, start with ten strokes up the penis, ten strokes down the penis, nine strokes up, nine strokes down, eight strokes up—all the way down to one.

To make the strokes even more erotic, use syncopation in your rhythm. Rather than stroking with an even beat as in a military march (1-2-3-4-5-6), jazz it up with an uneven beat like this:

1-2 — 3-4 — 5-6.

The sensations of this stroke can be fantastic on both a flaccid and an erect penis. When the penis is erect or semierect, your thumb and fingers surround the shaft on both the up and down movements.

When the penis is flaccid or semiflaccid, your hands surround the penis on the up movement. Then for the down movement, place the penis against his lower abdomen and slide your palms downward along the underneath side of the shaft. In both situations, remember to alternate one hand after the other.

As with all pleasuring methods, it is best to let go of orgasm goals. But should an ejaculation occur, as often happens with *The Countdown*, continue contact by letting your hands rest quietly on his genitals for a minute or so while he sinks into his afterglow.

For a variation, rest one of your palms on your partner's genitals and the other on his heart area. This is very comforting and helps to connect the sexual and love energies.

This would be a wonderful time to give a facial massage. It is a tender way to say "I love you." (*Cross*

References: Perhaps follow the suggestions for a facial massage in *Lingering in the Afterglow* (#5).)

Should you want more *Hole-in-the-Donut* strokes, the following chapter presents *The Cosmic Orifice* and *The Infinity Stroke*.

§ Please consult Appendix C.

15

The Gift of Pleasure

"A lovely, tender moment came when I was on top of him. He allowed me to touch him without touching me back. He was just receiving while I was touching his face, and neck, and chest, stroking my hands up and down his body.

"In the candlelight I could tell that he was enjoying what I was doing with him—bending over him and kissing his neck and running my hands through his hair.

"That he could allow me to do these things without doing something—some action—in return made me very loving toward him.

"Being receptive is not a discipline for him. It's the way he is sexually, and I appreciate it very much."

• *Male Genital Massage, Part II* [§] •

It is a beautiful gift we give to our lover when we allow ourselves to truly receive. If we allow ourselves to deeply feel our own pleasure while we are receiving erotic attentions, we may find our lover getting very aroused hearing, seeing, and feeling the response in our body.

If you are a man, allow yourself to really receive the following strokes and see what happens. Again lie

---

Kissing his neck and running my hands through his hair...

---

back, relax, and allow yourself to feel while your lover spreads oil over your body.

(*Cross References:* This is the second chapter on massage strokes for men's genitals. You may want to precede the following strokes with *The Hole in the Donut* (#14).)

∞ ∞ ∞

The Infinity Stroke

This stroke is easy to do, though a little tricky to learn. The most important part to remember is that your lover should always feel an *upward* stroking sensation.

Sit or kneel at your lover's right side. After applying lots of oil, embrace the base of the penile shaft with your left hand while your right hand makes a movement similar to the infinity sign: ∞.

Encircle the penis on the underneath side with your right palm in a fistlike shape. The thumb and index finger will be at the tip of the penis. Begin the stroke by gently squeezing and sliding upward toward the tip.

Just as your palm is about to come off the end of the penis, rotate your hand toward the left and down. Thus your palm encircles the penis with your little-finger area now near the tip of the head.

Without a stop in the flow, gently squeeze and slide upward toward the tip of the penis. This time when your palm is about to come off the end of the penis, you rotate your hand to the right and down. This puts you back in the beginning position. Your partner might enjoy an infinite number of repetitions.

Use plenty of oil. After a while you might ask if the stroke is becoming too intense.

The Cosmic Orifice

Now the snug, warm, lubricated orifice of your hand envelops the penis. To the recipient it feels as if his penis were thrusting continually forward, never having to pull back.

Curl each hand into a relaxed, fistlike shape. A small channel remains along the palm. The thumb and index-finger portion is on top.

Alternating your hands, begin a series of downward strokes along the head of the penis. In this stroke, your hands do not continue down the entire shaft. Stroke only the head and maybe an inch or so below. As your hand slides down past the head, immediately place it so that it is ready to begin again.

You might find this stroke difficult to do on a flaccid penis. Try some of the other strokes first.

Feelin' Good All Over
This stroke integrates the genitals with the rest of the body and can eroticize its entirety.

First connect the abdomen and the penis. One of your hands strokes up and down the penis while the other hand makes firm circular movements on your lover's abdomen. A variation for the second hand is to slide slowly back and forth across the waist.

Next try the breast area and the penis. With firm pressure, you can slide your palm across the breast toward the opposite shoulder. Then with your fingertip, delicately trace spiraling circles inward toward the nipple.

Now combine massaging the penis with strokes along the shoulders and neck where the muscles often store tension. Releasing this tension will probably be very pleasurable for your lover. Stroking his penis is also likely to be very pleasurable. According to some, putting the two together produces ecstasy.

On the shoulder and neck muscles, you can place a firm pressure with the flat part of your fingers and move your hand in small circles.

Perhaps slide the flat of your fingers up and down the muscles from the shoulder to the bottom of the head. Being careful not to put pressure on the throat area, try other strokes or develop new ones.

You can massage any other part of your lover's body while stroking his penis. Let *Feelin' Good All Over* be an exploration of sensations and feelings. Be open to pleasure enveloping his whole body. Be in contact with your own feelings that you have for your lover.

Let it be a lovely, tender moment of sharing the gift of pleasure.

§ Please consult Appendix C.

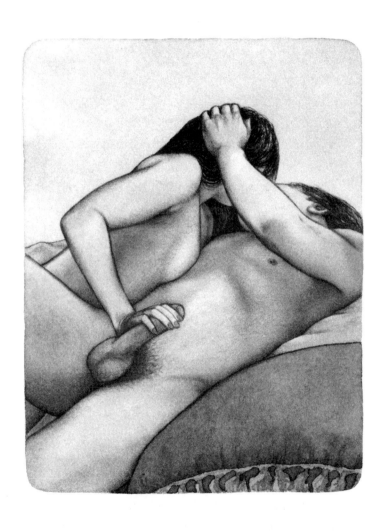

16

Down There

"Don't touch down there."

"Keep it clean down there."

We've all heard variations on these themes.

Most dolls are made without any "down theres."

"Down there" are our genitals and anus.

However, if we wish to have psychological and physical well-being, we must feel positive about all of our body.

I invite you to explore the following bathing. It can be both a relaxing and loving ceremony.

Should you have reservations about trying what may be a new experience, I encourage you to at least begin the ceremony. This chapter may be the most valuable of the book.

• *A Pelvic Bathing Ceremony* [§] •

These are the accessories you will need: a basin of very warm or hot water, soap (preferably liquid), an unscented massage oil, a washcloth, and a couple of towels.

(These instructions are written as if a man is the receiver.)

A quiet mood is always conducive. For me, Gregorian chants deepen the feeling. You might prefer other relaxing music.

You can use a padded floor or the bed. And placing a pillow underneath your lover's head may be comforting.

To begin, invite your partner to lie down with his pelvis on a towel. You will be sitting between his legs and facing him. If possible, sit with his legs resting on top of your outstretched legs. Perhaps a few pillows underneath you will make it easier.

When you are settled, dip the washcloth in and out of the hot water. Squeeze out the excess and drape the warmed cloth on the genital and anal areas. First, though, lift the penis and scrotum so that the cloth warms the sensitive underneath side.

To this special glow, you add the soothing touch of your palms resting on his abdomen. Feel his breathing. Perhaps inhaling and exhaling together, you deepen the sense of ceremony.

After a few minutes, allow your hands to ascend very slowly. Now mix some soap and water in them. As you remove the washcloth, begin to stroke the soap and water around his inner buttocks and anus.

(Regarding hemorrhoid conditions, if there is no pain, this bathing and massage would probably be

If we wish to have psychological and physical well-being, we must feel positive about *all* of our body.

fine as long as you are gentle. And when a woman is receiving, be careful not to stroke directly into the vagina. This might transfer organisms from the anal area.)

Let your hands move gracefully and slowly. Feel the exquisite sensations in your fingers. The medium of soap and water creates a serene mood.

When you feel inclined, use the warmed washcloth to remove the soap suds. Do not be concerned if you miss a few. And most of all, be gentle.

Now you turn to the medium of oil.

Warm several drops in your hands and alternating your hands, spread the oil upward from the base of the spine. (Remember to refrain from stroking into the vagina.)

After pouring more oil in your hands, slide them up his inner thighs, over the pelvis, and up the abdomen and chest as far as you can reach. Continuing your movement, slide down the sides of the torso, the pelvis, and the outer thighs. You can repeat this connecting stroke often.

As gracefully as possible, now lift his knees one at a time. Invite him to hold them in a relaxed manner near his chest.

After adding more oil to your hands, begin stroking his buttocks.

Next, imagine a line from just below his scrotum down to the base of his spine. (For a woman, start below the vaginal opening.) With your thumb pads pointing toward each other, place them at the top of this line. Apply a firm but not harsh pressure and slide them outward in a separating movement. Repeat this stroke along a series of points down the line.

Throughout this ceremony, I recommend not penetrating the anal orifice. Allow your lover to relax and feel many delicate sensations.

Next is an exquisite stroke. Using plenty of oil, very slowly trace small circles near the anal orifice with a single finger pad.

Now begin firm strokes from your lover's buttocks up the backs of his thighs. When you feel ready, very slowly lower his legs back down with subtle rocking movements. Very slowly.

Similar to the beginning of the ceremony, give several gentle connecting strokes up the thighs to the chest and back down the sides. Perhaps you can also reach up to his shoulders and then stroke down his arms and hands. If possible, stroke your hands down his legs and off the toes. This massaging will reintegrate his "down there" with the rest of his body.

For a final touch, again bring your hands to rest in silence on his abdomen.

After a few minutes, lift your hands and slide out from underneath his legs. Though this is difficult, be as graceful as possible.

Now quietly cuddle up next to your lover.

Softly embrace.

And feel.

§ Please consult Appendix C.

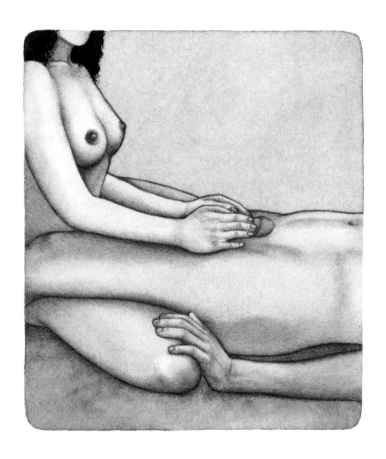

17

A Man's G Spot?

Does a man have a G spot?

Seeing G-spot stimulation result in wilder movements and moaning for a woman, a man might be wishing something like this were available in his body also.

Well, wish no more. Men have a G spot.

Oops…perhaps I should qualify that. Men have in their body a similar place that is a possible source of deep, sexual pleasure.

Whether it is equivalent to the female G spot is not certain. I leave that to other sexologists and to anatomists to argue.

It may be more accurate to say this: There is a place in the male body that responds similarly as the female G spot. Both "spots" are approximately in the same place and both can be stimulated by finger pads.

And both women and men report similarly about the sensations. Often at first there is a feeling of a need to urinate. Later, as sexual arousal becomes more intense, the pleasure seems to emanate from deep in the core of the pelvis—a sensation quite different than from penile or clitoral stimulation.

Though men can explore their "G spot" on their own, it might be more effective and more exciting to share this with a lover.

• *Deep Pelvic Massage* [§] •

The place I have been describing is the prostate gland. Your first thought may be that this will be something like the doctor's examination. Believe me, this is very different. Physicians are not trained to give pleasure.

The main accessory is a lubricant, perhaps one that is water based. You might also use vinyl medical examination gloves if you are concerned about hygiene or communicable conditions.

The giver will need to have at least one finger with a short, smooth fingernail. If this is not the case, the receiver could substitute his own finger in these instructions, assuming the fingernail is suitable. If there are hemorrhoid conditions, it may be best to consult a physician first.

As a prelude, take a sensuous bath or shower to-gether. Or you might prefer the soothing pelvic bath-ing ritual presented in the previous chapter. Afterward the receiver lies back, relaxes, and simply feels.

The following instructions assume the giver is massaging from the recipient's right side.

∞ ∞ ∞

First stroke and caress your lover's body with oil. After a while focus more attention on his penis. Apply even more oil here.

As he becomes highly aroused, your right hand begins stroking the whole length of the underside of the penile shaft. Your left hand massages his penis throughout this and the remaining strokes.

When his feelings become more intense, concen-trate your right-hand movements on the area just be-low the pubic bone and above the anal opening. Using the flat of your fingers in a paddlelike shape, put a firm pressure on this "cavity." Now make small circles so that his skin moves over the muscles beneath.

Later, should the experience become too uncom-fortable, this is an excellent stroke to which to return.

Next make very delicate circles with a fingertip pad around the anal orifice. There are many sensitive nerve endings you can stimulate.

If you are finding it difficult to reach your lover's pelvic floor, you can ask him to bring his right knee upward so you can brace it with your chest.

Whenever he becomes "really turned on," your longest finger (with a smooth, short fingernail) begins to enter the anal orifice. Until the sphincter muscles become accustomed to this touch, your lover may find the sensations intense.

There are many sensitive nerve endings you can stimulate.

So rather than sliding your finger directly in, begin a gentle, rocking motion. Giving small, gradual stretches, you invite the muscles to relax. Remember to use plenty of oil.

When your finger is in full length, try a "come here" stroking with the finger pad against the tissues on the upper area, at twelve o'clock. Here is the approximate area of the prostate gland. Depending on the length of your finger, you may feel a firmer, spongy tissue a little different than surrounding tissues.[1]

You may feel nothing with your finger. What is really important is what your lover feels in his body. If it is deeply pleasurable, forget about anatomy.

Explore other stroking movements. If it feels good, you are doing it correctly.

Perhaps you would like to combine this massage with coitus. (Have fun finding in which positions this is possible.) And if you think you would like to receive a similar, deep pelvic massage, ask your lover to reciprocate at some time.

(Before making contact with the vaginal area, remember to wash with soap and water any parts of your bodies that have had contact with anal areas.)

After your explorations, share verbally about your experiences together.

This may have stimulated many intimate feelings of tenderness and trust.

§ Please consult Appendix C.

[1] For further information, see *Anal Pleasure and Health* by Jack Morin, Ph.D. (Burlingame, California: Down There Press, 1981).

18

The S Spot and Other Pleasure Resorts

"Oh no, not another push-button-sex point."

"Why not?" is my response. The clitoris, the G spot, the head of the penis, the prostate, the nipples—these are only the current hit parade. Some of the places not yet discovered by the media are the left triceps muscle, between the shoulder blades, the right thigh, and four o'clock, eight o'clock, and 5:30 in the vagina. (Oh yes, let's not forget Wagner's "Prelude" and "Liebestod" from *Tristan and Isolde* for the mind spot.)

I agree that a lover does not like to be a machine pushed here to respond one way and poked there to be programmed another way.

But here's my theory: If the popularity list becomes long enough, we will get tired of trying to memorize and perform every point. Sooner or later, we'll just throw out the list and go back to spontaneously joyful sexual play over the whole body.

∞ ∞ ∞

At the risk of encouraging push-button sex, I would like to introduce two new "spots" to explore: the S spot and the BP spot. As far as I know, these have never been written about before.

• *The S Spot* •

The S spot is a potentially sexually stimulating area on the neck.

After I began to teach this "spot" in my Sensate Therapy trainings to sex therapists, the students affectionately referred to it as the Stubbs spot, or S spot.

When stroked, the recipient might experience it as an enjoyable neck massage, a painful neck massage (because of too much pressure), or a pleasurable sensation in the genital area.

Customarily, when a sensation is felt in the genitals, it is characterized as sexual and frequently as extremely arousing. Unfortunately, it is almost exclusively women who report this sensation.

To locate the S spot on your lover, you will be looking for a small, tight muscle generally less than half an inch to either side of the tips of the spine. Although most frequently about one inch down from the base of the skull, it could vary from the base of the skull itself down to three or four inches along the spine of the neck.

More important than which muscle is the muscle's feel. You are more likely to find the S spot on a muscle that is tight, often like a very thin rope.

The clitoris, the G spot, the head of the penis, the prostate, the nipples— these are only the current hit parade.

To stimulate the spot, you "twang" the "rope" with the soft pads of your fingertips. This is sort of like playing a guitar or string bass.

Before you just walk over to your lover and start twanging her neck, first move into a sensuous mood— the longer you take, the better. Unexpected grabbing and stroking of a clitoris or penis is unlikely to have an erotic effect. The same is true for the S spot.

Also, be very careful not to put too much pressure and not to massage the sides of the neck. These may create pain rather than pleasure.

By no means do all women respond sexually to neck twanging. So be open to giving a good neck massage only. The most important thing is that you have shared your caring attentions with each other.

• *The BP Spot* § •

The BP spot, or Base of Penis spot, is for men. On the underneath side of the penile shaft, it is an area varying from about the level of the scrotum to the bottom of the pubic bone.

When the giver combines massaging this area with stroking the penis, a man may feel as if he is in heaven.

More accurately, he may have a sensation that feels as though every part of the genitals—from the tip of the penis to its roots inside the pelvis—is being held and stroked at once.

It is less likely that a man will discover the BP spot while stimulating himself. What may be best for the recipient is to lie back, relax, and give occasional feedback while a lover does the stroking.

∞ ∞ ∞

Perhaps using massage oil, begin with strokes and caresses on your partner's chest, abdomen, genitals, and thighs. Invite him to close his eyes.

After a while, focus more strokes on his genitals. (*Cross References:* Try the male genital strokes from *The Hole in the Donut* (#14) and *The Gift of Pleasure* (#15).)

When he becomes highly aroused, let your left hand stroke up and down along the shaft and head of his penis. (These instructions assume you are on his right side.)

Form your right-hand fingers into a flat, paddle-like shape. With your hand parallel to the penis, your finger "paddle" strokes along the base of the penis in the BP spot area. Stroking as far back as the anus—although it may feel good—is beyond the BP spot.

Your right-hand pressure is to be only firm enough to move his skin up and down over the tissues just beneath his skin. Either giving too much pressure or sliding your fingers over the skin may not produce the desirable effect.

As with any other "spot," you and your lover may find nothing. Perhaps try further explorations at another time.

In the meantime, continue doing whatever feels good. Pleasure is what's important, not the buttons.

§ Please consult Appendix C.

19

Soothing Vibrations

When I was a child, I would usually get a flattop at the barber's. In this style the hair is cut short on the top—short enough to stand straight up in a flat plane.

There were two great things about getting this flattop. First, the barber needed to use a special electric clipper. I would hear a quiet hum. Then would come a flood of tingling tickles across my scalp and down my back. As the razor trimmed, I would try to sit very still to feel the ripples from each erect hair strand. I was in heaven.

After the haircut would come the second great part. Sometimes the barber would slip a black metal vibrator on his hand and massage my scalp.

This was rapture. I secretly wanted to "ummmm" in pleasure.

But even at a young age I sensed that little boys (and men) do not make those sounds in public.

Luckily, as an adult I now have both a vibrator and a lover who likes to massage my scalp. And she loves to hear me moan.

• *Vibrators* •

Generally there are four categories of home vibrators. The first three are plug-in models and the fourth is battery operated. (The home electronics industry is very creative, so new varieties may appear.)

First is the kind that barbers had when I was growing up. These are fairly heavy and strap on the back side of your hand. Their advantage is that they make

This was rapture.
I wanted to "ummmm"
in pleasure.

your fingers the vibrating instrument, allowing direct contact with your lover.

But be very careful. The straps can get caught in chest and pubic hair. Also, many people find this type of vibrator too noisy and painful on their hand after a short while.

The second type of vibrator has a shape similar to a handheld hair dryer. It comes with several attachments for different parts of the body. This and the next type are most popular with lovers.

The third variety is also handheld but cylinder shaped with a vibrating bulb on the end about two inches in diameter. It may come with low and high speeds. A newer variation on this model has the added attraction of two vibrating bulbs.

The fourth type is the plastic battery-operated vibrator. It exists in a wide range of shapes, many of which are designed explicitly for sexual play. Unfortunately, many of these vibrators are poorly manufactured. And their batteries die—just when you need them the most.

• *Soothing Vibrations* •

Once you have selected a vibrator, here are some suggestions on where and how to use it.

The most appreciated places are usually the muscles connecting the neck and shoulders, the muscles running down along the spine, and the lower back. If the mood is erotic, genitals and breasts often respond to sensitively applied vibration.[§] (There will be more on these in the next chapter.) The feet, hands, and scalp are other favorites.

When you are first learning to use a vibrator, a good idea is to first try it on yourself. Experiment with location, angle, and degree of pressure. This will give you some good clues to what might feel good to your partner.

But first, there are some important cautions. On varicose veins and inflamed or injured areas, let a medical or health professional advise what is best.

For bony areas such as the head, apply lighter pressure and perhaps skip the edges and tips of bones.

If ticklishness results, try a firmer pressure. Whenever there is discomfort, do not persist. Go to a new area.

Except for the kind that straps on the back of your hand, you can place the vibrator directly on your partner.

An excellent variation is to place the vibrator's head on the back of your hand as it rests directly on your partner. This will soften the intensity and often spread the vibrations over a larger surface.

If the vibrations are too intense, another possibility is to place a folded cloth between your lover and the vibrator. Experiment. Be open to feedback.

The pressure can vary from a light tickle to a firm contact. You can leave the vibrator stationary or slide it along or across a muscle.

For a unique sensation, place enough pressure to sort of "hook" the skin and muscle. Then without sliding across the skin, move the vibrator in different directions from its original contact point. You may find a line of electric tingles.

Be open to all possible responses from your lover. Tense muscles may let go. She or he may be energized to go dancing—or soothed to sleep.

A few humming attentions go a long way to let your lover know that you care.

§ Please consult Appendix C.

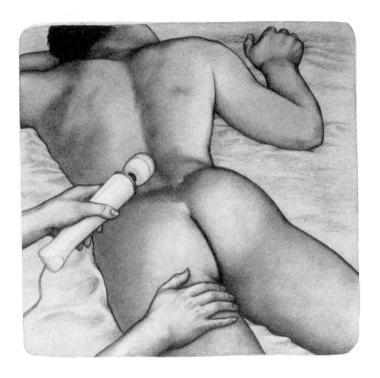

20

Erotic Vibrations

This is a true story although the name is fictitious to ensure confidentiality.

I have a close friend, Kathryn, who loves vibrators. She has battery-operated ones, plug-in ones, big ones, small ones, fur-covered ones.

Owning her own business, she finds at the end of a long day that the vibrators give beneficial relief to her tense neck and shoulder muscles.

Kathryn also likes to use the vibrators when she masturbates and plays with her lover. She has become quite adept—shall we say "an expert"—at the art of good vibrations.

But there is something Kathryn does not like: going to the dentist.

So she came up with a bright idea. Why not take a vibrator to her next dental appointment? Fortunately her dentist agreed to try it.

Tenderly hold the nipple with the vibrating index finger and thumb.

Once in the dental chair, Kathryn simply placed her humming vibrator over the clothing covering her pubic bone. When she felt the vibrations building strong, pleasurable, sexual feelings in her body, she indicated to her dentist to begin drilling.

The concept is simple. Both vibrators and dental drills vibrate. By shifting her focus to desirable, sexual sensations, Kathryn was able to displace undesirable experiences from the drilling.

Dental science took a bold, new step that afternoon. Kathryn went home feeling good. This time there was no postdrilling trauma.

Such a procedure is based on sound psychological reasoning. Too bad the dental profession would view it as "unethical behavior."

• *Erotic Vibrations* § •

If you are interested at home in shifting your focus to pleasurable feelings, here are some tips for you and your lover.

Most of all, bring an attitude of exploration to your vibrator play. You may find places on your lover's body never before considered erogenous.

Always be gentle and be open to suggestions. Your partner can feel from the inside what is happening in his or her body. (You might want to refer to the previous chapter for general vibrator suggestions.)

If your partner's response is neutral, turn off the vibrator and relax with some caresses and kisses. Postpone further explorations for a more loving and erotic mood.

Nipples

Both women's and men's nipples often respond to vibrations. First try a soft, direct contact on the nipple. Compare that with the following. If possible, grip the head of the vibrator between your index and middle finger. Then tenderly hold the nipple with the vibrating index finger and thumb of the same hand.

Clitoris

Generally the clitoris is a woman's most responsive area for a vibrator. You might begin here by placing your fingers between the vibrator and the clitoral area. Varying the pressure, also explore up and down along the labia.

Penis

Many men find wonderful surprises when a vibrator hums up against the frenulum, which is the inverted "V" area on the underneath side of the head of the penis. This is a "must try" for men who insist vibrators have no erotic effect on them.

Perineum

Another exciting area for many women and men is from immediately behind the genitals to near the bottom of the spine. Many nerve endings here come alive during sexual arousal.

As you slide your vibrator along this area, be careful not to move microorganisms from the anus to the vagina. You and your partner might enjoy a sensuous bath or shower first. Another option is to vibrate through a small towel that remains stationary on the pelvic floor. Also, be cautious with vibrators on scrotums. With some types of vibrators, it might be very painful.

In your own erotic investigations, you may have found other exciting places. Play with them too. And don't forget between the toes.

∞ ∞ ∞

Portable Vibrations

Certain vibrators make for exquisite surprises. Plastic, battery-operated vibrators are ideal in dark movie theaters or anywhere you can not use plug-in models.

Made especially for lovers, they can be inserted in the vagina, in the anus, or around the penis. (A word of caution: Before inserting into an orifice, make certain the vibrator is clean and structurally sturdy. Also, in the anal area *be very careful not to let any object slip entirely past the sphincter muscles.*)

One portable model preferred by several women I know has two branches. One is inserted in the vagina and the other, shorter branch snuggles against the clitoris.

If you are wondering about your lover's next birthday or anniversary gift...

Good Vibrations Hug

Let's end the chapter with a vibrating beginning.

Fully clothed and standing up, invite your lover to share a hug. Nestle your turned-on vibrator into a comfortable position between your pubic areas. Then hug for five minutes.

Don't let go. Don't fall down.

And make certain there aren't any urgent appointments following this hug—you would probably be late.

§ Please consult Appendix C.

21

The Land of Whipped Cream and Honey

"For about two hours—that's how long he did it." This is a woman telling how her lover pleasured her one evening in a movie theater.

"As we entered the dark hallway from the lobby, he kissed me. It was brief and very exciting.

"Then as we watched the film, he began to stroke my breasts. And he didn't move on to doing anything else. I remember kissing a little with my hand snuggled between his thighs. Throughout the movie he continued to fondle and caress my breasts —in a way that no one could see. Oh, I was so lubricated from being aroused for so long and not having sex. When the movie was finally over, we hurried to his van in the parking lot, closed the curtains, and made love."

• *Breast Massage* •

Many women and men find that their breasts respond to long interludes of stroking and kissing. The following strokes, unfortunately, will be too obvious for a dark movie theater.

Get some massage oil, light a candle, and invite your lover to lie down. Sitting beside her, set a sensual

---

As we entered the dark hallway from the lobby, he kissed me.

---

mood with slow caresses over all of the body. (This chapter is written as if the recipient is female, though men equally love to receive it.)

When she is ready for a focus on her breasts, move beside her right arm and warm some oil in your hands.

Taking Flight

Your first stroke, *Taking Flight*, begins with your right hand on her rib cage just below and to the right of her right breast. Your fingers and palm are pointing toward her left shoulder.

Slowly and without pressure, slide your hand up and across the outer side of the breast and nipple as if your hand were a plane taking off diagonally toward the left shoulder. Applying much pressure or sliding in other directions may be uncomfortable for her.

Before your right hand lifts off, repeat the same stroke with your left hand. Continue this pattern ten or more times.

There is no necessity to do these strokes for two hours. You may, however, find your lover more responsive if you let everything be slow and easy.

The Spiral

The Spiral is next. With your fingertip circling the outer part of your lover's breast, delicately and slowly trace a spiral inwardly. Eventually your finger will spiral up to the nipple. After many repetitions of the stroke, ask her which speed and pressure pleases her most. Also explore which direction of circling feels best.

The Spokes Stroke

For *The Spokes Stroke*, imagine the nipple as the axis in a wheel with spokes radiating out from the center. Here you use the pads of your index fingers and thumbs. Give a gentle squeeze to the skin at the base of the axis and slide outward (in opposite directions) along a spoke. Repeat on all the spokes.

The Axis

Following with *The Axis*, lovingly squeeze the base of the nipple between the pads of your index finger and thumb. Then slide up and off the nipple, alternating your hands, one immediately after the other.

Now follow the same sequence on your lover's left breast. If you prefer not to move your body to her left side, just modify *Taking Flight* by using a pulling motion from her left rib cage up toward her right shoulder.

• Oral Strokes •

If the taste of the massage oil is unpleasant to you, gently wipe it off with a towel before giving oral strokes.

(*Cross References:* In earlier chapters there are a wide variety of oral massage strokes, many of which could be deliciously applied to your lover's breasts. See *Lolita's Lips* (#8) and *The Big, Bad Wolf* (#9).)

There are many possibilities, but here's one I saved especially for this chapter—it's my lover's favorite. This is something we all did as babies.

Encircle your lips around the areola. With the nipple between your tongue and upper palate, make a sucking motion. If the suction is with the lips only, the sensation is good. But it is truly exquisite when the nipple is farther inside the mouth between the tongue and upper palate.

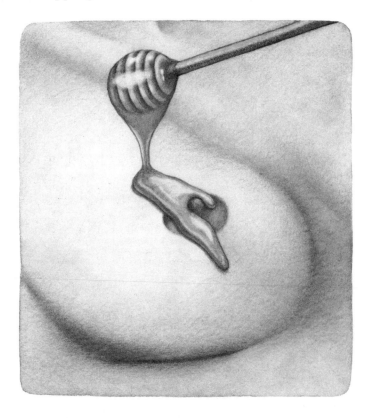

There's a secret to this. Never entirely release your suction. The nipple moves back and forth, but always keep at least a minimal suction.

Now for an epicurean variation—sort of an adult version of breast-feeding. Gently spread whipped cream or honey over your lover's breast after warning that there might be a chilling sensation at first. Then savor.

It may not be so clear who is having the most pleasure.

You may find yourselves moved—after losing track of time—to partake of other passions. Be certain, though, never to get sweet ingredients inside the vagina.

∞ ∞ ∞

Receiving such erotic delights may strike your fancy. Should your lover be willing, he or she could reciprocate, experimenting with and adapting the strokes.

As a recipient now, you just lie back and enjoy. This is the land of whipped cream and honey.

22

Naughty but Nice

Fantasy games are fun. Being grown-up doesn't mean we can't play anymore. The games are different, that's all.

As one of my seminar participants suggested, "It's reminiscent of high school days, where it builds up anticipation. Like being slowly undressed at the drive-in movies."

A close woman friend shared her and her lover's fantasy. "He likes for me to wear high heels to bed. He actually comes along with me to buy them."

Being naughty is a nice way to spice up your love life. Doing something out of the ordinary—if your lover is in accordance—can bring thrills not soon forgotten. Doing what you usually do but in an uncommon setting can heat up a lukewarm evening to a fever, as it did for this woman in a sauna:

"It was very steamy and hot. It was languid. I remember sitting on the bench with one knee up and the other leg open. I could see my lover's eyes looking at my vulva. It really turned me on."

Here are a few more fantasies you can try.

• Fantasy Games for Lovers •

Prom Night

Reviving events from the past presents a treasure chest of possibilities. The high school prom is one of my favorites.

With this one, let your imagination run wild through your memories. What did everyone wear to the high school dances? What was your hair style? What color were your socks?

Once you and your lover have your lists, phone around to rent or purchase what you need. Maybe even borrow a car that was popular back then. See if you can get your hair styled à la high school for the grand occasion. And of course, don't forget the corsage.

If you and your lover live together, make arrangements for the woman to be picked up elsewhere, reminiscent of a previous lifestyle. (A contemporary variation could be for the woman to pick the man up.)

Maybe there's an "oldies but goodies" dance to attend. If not, select another dance spot with a live band. Pretend it really is prom night.

And don't worry about the other people. If you are living it up, they will enjoy it too.

Afterward, you might want to go park. Only necking and fondling, let your passions build in the car. Feel

Women do it, men do it.

the excitement of not being able to take your clothes off.

You might check into a motel. For suspense, take off marriage rings, use different last names, act nervous, and pay in cash in advance.

In your room, one of you might play resistant while the other pursues.

This is my scenario, but any variation on the theme would be fine. What's most important is that you and your lover have fun.

The Strip

Women do it, men do it. The striptease has titillated humankind for centuries.

This may take a little preparation, but you don't have to be a trained dancer. Just strut your stuff. Really put yourself into it.

Select some good strip or blues music—something you can grind your pelvis to.

Get a pair of very sexy underwear, maybe a silk scarf. Be creative. (Tight jeans, though, are difficult to remove gracefully. But then it might be exciting with a little assistance from your audience of one.)

There's no need to practice beforehand. If you want to get a few ideas, watch some male or female stripteasers on video or in a live performance.

Making your presentation a surprise might be best. Let your lover know you have a special evening planned. You might begin with a candlelight dinner and champagne. Whatever you do, set an erotic ambience. Your gift is the giving of yourself, not just the taking off of your clothes.

When the beat of the music begins, let it move your body. Forget about performing. Just express yourself. Look into your lover's eyes. Tease. Your partner can touch, but not too much.

Let the evening unfold.

∞　∞　∞

Some fantasy games you act out. Some you whisper in your lover's ear.

They might be planned or might be spontaneous.

Consensus is crucial. Always present the fantasy game as an invitation. If it does not interest your lover, wait for another time.

There are many provocative possibilities for acting-out games. One of you is the doctor, the other a patient coming in for a very private examination. Or one of you is the teacher giving a special after-class tutorial.

Perhaps play hitchhiker. One of you actually stands on the street, signaling thumb extended. Pretending you are strangers, one naughtily seduces the other.

The fantasies are endless. Just pick one.

Let your gaze linger and your touch tease. Savor the stirring in your body.

See where it leads you.

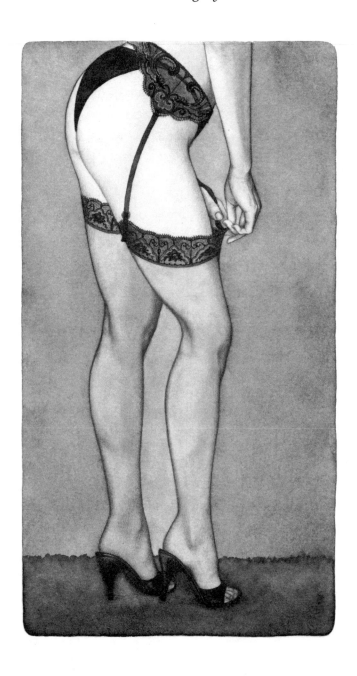

23

The Three-Hands Massage

"For me to have a really good orgasm, it's a mixture of getting really relaxed and feeling the sensation building. The more I relax, the deeper my feelings go. This is a really fulfilling part of sex."

This woman expresses what is true for many of us, both men and women. When we carry the excess baggage of tensions, worries, and other body/mind distractions, we cannot fully feel our pleasure.

So why not combine the soothing, relaxing qualities of massage with the intensifying passions of coitus? This will give you a new adventure called a *Three-Hands Massage*."

In this experience, it is essential that one lover gives while the other remains completely relaxed.

Should the receiving partner become involved in giving back, orchestrating the events, or thrusting the pelvis frequently, many qualities will be lost. With inner calm, subtle ripples of pleasure can feel like waves.

• *Manual Massage with Coitus* [§] •

You will need a quiet space without interruptions and either a bed or a sheet with padding for the floor. Soft music and a candle are also nice.

For oil, the best selection may be an unscented, pure vegetable oil. However, if the woman's vagina is sensitive to the oil, you can just as easily give a *Three-Hands Massage* without oil inside the vagina. If you are using a condom because of concerns about pregnancy or communicable conditions, be certain not to allow on the condom any oil containing vegetable or petroleum products. These deteriorate the latex.

It is usually best to give fifteen or more minutes of manual massage before using your penis or vagina as the third hand.

Never rush. Allow the feelings to build. Hard or rapid pelvic thrusting is not necessary. Let go of orgasm as the goal. If an orgasm does occur for either of you, fine. Enjoy it.

Use any massage strokes you like or discover.

Be open to wherever this leads you.

Man Giving

With your partner lying face down, help her to relax by massaging her back.

After caressing, stroking, and perhaps kissing her neck, shoulders, and back, gracefully bring your thighs to straddle her thighs and buttocks. You can spread oil on your abdomen, genitals, and thighs. This makes the contact between your bodies exquisitely smooth.

Whenever you reposition your body, continue stroking your lover as much as possible. Let it be like slow dancing, swaying to the music.

The more I relax, the deeper my feelings go.

With your hands flowing and thighs sliding, gradually enter her vagina. Let time disappear. The slower the entry, the more arousing the pleasure.

Now blend the movement of your pelvis with the soothing touch of your hands on her back, the muscles along her spine, and possibly her shoulders. You may be able to include the calves and feet.

There is more to come. At some point, invite your lover to turn over.

Lift her knees toward her chest and again slowly slide your penis into her vagina. Perhaps sitting on your heels, lower her legs onto your thighs.

Slowly rocking your pelvis, now let your hands stroke her thighs, torso, and arms. Remind her to let her whole body melt into the bed beneath should she become highly active. The more she relaxes, the more pleasurable sensations she will feel.

Woman Giving

With the woman as the active partner, the positions are different but the dance is the same. The movements are slow and graceful. The recipient remains receptive rather than active.

Begin with your lover lying on his back. Face him with your thighs straddling his pelvis.

When you are ready to envelop your lover's penis with your vagina, you might first stroke his penis against your clitoris and labia. This is often a stirring experience for both partners whether the penis is flaccid or erect. Then very, very slowly lower your pelvis, dancing an exotic dance, building both your passions.

To stroke his legs and feet, simply reposition yourself to face his feet while continuing to straddle his pelvis.

To massage his back, shift positions so that your partner is now lying on top of you. If his weight is too intense, he can brace himself on his elbows and forearms. Since this position affords few massage possibilities, you might forgo it in a three-hands massage. However, it may be very nice for other forms of lovemaking.

∞ ∞ ∞

There is no specific way to end a *Three-Hands Massage*.

What is most important is to linger, letting the glow brighten. Stimulating your lover's genitals with your genitals while massaging other parts can spread erotic pleasures to every cell of his or her body.

Be open to any possibility.

§ Please consult Appendix C.

24

Love/Sex/God

Couples in one of my seminars were sharing about their tender moments: "After we've made love, we lie there breathing together, not talking. We hold each other, and it seems like we disappear, like we have turned into love."

"I like opening my eyes and looking at my lover," added a woman. "It adds closeness."

∞ ∞ ∞

As meditation has become more accepted, many lovers have brought these techniques into their sex play.

Quieting the mind and relaxing the body can be paths to fuller sexual expression. Deepening our awareness, we can feel ripples of pleasure through our whole body. We touch not only with our lips, genitals, and hands—we touch with our heart.

Some sexual meditation methods are very involved and far beyond the scope of this chapter. But there are two valuable techniques you can easily explore.

Though variations of these have probably at some time been a part of religious rituals, you need not believe in a god or a religious system to practice them. In fact, a rigidity of belief could even interfere.

If, after exploring these meditations, you find them irrelevant or distracting, drop them. Bringing additional burdens to the bed will never make lovemaking more sensuous.

•   *Unison Breathing*   •

In *Unison Breathing*, you and your lover simply breathe at the same pace. As one inhales, the other inhales. As one exhales, the other exhales.

At first you may find this pattern mechanical. As you become more accustomed, an effortless blending of movement may result. Your breathing can become a quiet dance.

You will most likely lose all sense of time. Lovers speak of merging, becoming One. You might experience these.

To begin, lie down with your lover, preferably

nude. You may want to cover yourselves so that you do not become chilled.

Position yourselves so that you can feel the expansion and releasing of each other's breathing. It may be best to rest on your sides, one behind the other. An

---

We hold each other and it seems like we disappear, like we have turned into love.

---

alternative is to embrace face to face, maybe one on top of the other.

Once you find a position that will be comfortable for ten to thirty minutes, begin to focus on your breathing. Though it is not necessary to use any specific breathing pattern, you might find slower, fuller breathing easier to feel. All you do is match your breath with your lover's.

For the first few sessions, I suggest setting aside at least ten minutes to allow your rhythms to synchronize. (But don't watch the clock.)

Once you become accustomed to *Unison Breathing,* you can use it before, during, or after sex. As it calms your mind, you may begin to feel the more subtle pleasures. Experiment to see how it might enrich your sensual and sexual life.

• *Eye Gazing* •

With *Eye Gazing*, you and your lover look softly in the direction of each other's eyes.

This is not staring or sharply focusing. Rather, it is more like looking with your peripheral vision. In a sense, you look at the air or energy between your eyes and your lover.

Without attempting to direct or to influence, allow yourselves simply to be together. With this method, interfering expectations and performances can melt away.

You might choose a left-eye-to-left-eye gaze. Another possibility is to focus on your lover's "third eye," the area between and slightly above the eyes. Experiment with the options, perhaps in separate sessions.

At first you may feel like smiling or giggling. This may break the mood, but do not get upset if it happens. Simply return to the soft, neutral gaze.

After you gaze for several minutes, you may begin to notice what appears to be changes in the shape of your lover's face. This is quite common and can be a distraction if you become involved in the whys and interpretations. Simply continue in the quietness and stillness.

Especially suitable before having sex, *Eye Gazing*

may bring more loving qualities to the way you make love. You may feel a deeper connection.

To begin, set aside at least five minutes. Fifteen minutes would be even better. Sit opposite your lover, perhaps on pillows on a bed or on chairs. Whichever method you use, be certain that both of you are comfortable.

Decide whether you will use the left-eye-to-left-eye or the third-eye method. Then take a moment to go inside yourselves with your eyes closed. Eye gazing begins when both you and your lover have opened your eyes.

After you become familiar with both the *Unison Breathing* and the *Eye Gazing*, combine them. This can be a richly rewarding experience.

Allow your feelings to unfold. These meditations can open new avenues.

Let your moments together become sacred.

(*Cross References:* Both of these meditations might be joined with other techniques in *Romantic Interludes*. You could begin with *Eye Gazing*. After your explorations, perhaps cuddle with a *Unison Breathing*.)

APPENDICES

Appendix A

Theoretical Frameworks:

Sexual Health, Sensate Therapy, and Tantra

Here are some mind cookies.

When you are feeling academically inclined, perhaps read the following. However, simply knowing more conceptual information is unlikely to make anyone more sensuous. In fact, being "stuck in our head" is probably the greatest inhibitor of sensuous experiences.

Yet, abstract thinking is as valuable a human function as is touching. What we need is a healthy balance between the two.

Pathology Model vs. Wellness Model

When we are ill, traditionally we turn to medicine and psychotherapy, which specialize in pathology. The focus is the diagnosis and cure of illness. Here health is defined as the absence of illness.

Reappearing in the last three decades, the field of holistic health has a different emphasis. The elimination of an illness is only a part of the process.

A comparison of the two models follows.[1]

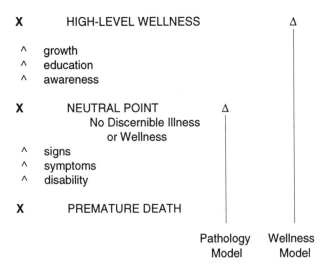

On this continuum, traditional medicine and

psychotherapy generally attempt to get us up to the "neutral point" of no discernible illness or wellness.

The wellness model does not stop there. Rather, the intention is to be in a state of high-level wellness, which means "giving good care to your physical self, using your mind constructively, expressing your emotions effectively, being creatively involved with those around you, being concerned about your physical and psychological environment and becoming aware of other levels of consciousness."[2]

Romantic Interludes is written from the perspective that nurturing and appreciating the senses are an integral part of creating wellness. Sensitively sharing the gifts described in this book can be an important contribution to your and your partner's well-being.

• *Sex Therapy* •

While *Romantic Interludes* does not specifically attempt to resolve sexual problems, many of the techniques are applicable in a therapeutic setting.

What most of us think of as contemporary sex therapy is actually a synthesis of four approaches: psychoanalysis, marital therapy, behavior therapy, and sensate focus exercises.[3]

In psychoanalysis the goal is to resolve unconscious conflicts through insight. Treatment of a sexual dysfunction is through long-term, in-depth, individual analysis.

Marital therapy, focusing on a couple's relationship, attempts to resolve unrecognized destructive interactions. In this model, sexual difficulties are usually considered to be a symptom of underlying conflicts.

In behavior therapy, we turn to observable behavior rather than examining the unconscious and other intrapsychic processes. There is no attempt to understand early traumatic events. The assumption is that like adaptive behaviors, maladaptive behaviors are learned. One can learn desirable sexual behaviors through conditioning procedures.

The fourth component is sensate focus exercises. Coined by William Masters, M.D., and Virginia Johnson, sensate focus means to focus on sensations. The inability to do this is an integral factor in many sexual dysfunctions.

To more fully understand sensate focus and other sensate processes, I propose the following theoretical framework. Within a pathology model, sensate processes would be titled "sensate therapy," and within a wellness model, "sensate awareness."

• *Sensate Therapy* •

Sensate therapy is a system of processes which employ the experience of sensate stimuli.

The system can include 1) relaxation procedures, 2) sensate focusing exercises, 3) sensual massage, and 4) nurturing rituals.

The general purpose of such processes is to expand our willingness and ability to experience our senses.

"Senses" commonly refers to a five-sense system of touching, tasting, smelling, seeing, and hearing. Modern science gives us a more extensive list, including sense receptors for heat, cold, and muscle movement. To go beyond the mind/body dualism of Western approaches, I would add, as does Buddhist psychology, the mental functions, such as thinking and imagining. Sucking on a lemon and imagining sucking on a lemon, for example, are equally "real" experiences.

"Sensate" connotes perception, consciousness, awareness. "Experience" refers to a preconceptual and preverbal state. In an experience there is a conscious awareness of perception. There is no necessity to conceptualize or verbalize the conceptualization. Moreover, the process of conceptualizing and verbalizing has a pervasive tendency to take one out of the actual experience.

Sensate therapy is especially applicable for sexual dysfunctions characterized by limited sensory perception and a lack of appreciation of the sensory experience. The understanding of one's sexual resistances (as pursued in psychoanalysis and marital therapy) is valuable, but the ability to fully experience sensations may still need to be rehabilitated. And while behavior therapy can increase sexual response and functioning, it does not necessarily enhance creativity. My observation is that sensate therapy is especially effective in increasing spontaneity and explorative factors crucial in a loving expression of sensuality, sexuality, and intimacy.

(Any attempt to characterize a school of thought is of course an oversimplification, especially since individual practitioners are involved on a daily basis in the evolution of theoretical structures. My intent here is to generalize the tendencies within these models.)

• *Principles* •

There are three principles which define a sensate approach methodology: receptivity, relaxation response, and present-time experience.

Receptivity means nonperformance and nondemand. In either a giving or a receiving role, there would be no psychological attachment to the outcome of one's actions. Unfortunately, it is easy to slip into performing in sexual behavior. We have an image of how we should be and we strive to live up to it. We might also communicate subtle demands for our partner to respond in a particular way.

Receptivity is not the same as passivity. Receptivity requires awareness and choice—very different from "giving up" and nonchoice submissiveness.

While this principle focuses on nonattachment to

a specified outcome, setting goals or directions is quite suitable. In fact, creating goals is often an extremely valuable part of the personal growth process. But when we strive to achieve a desired outcome, we miss many valuable experiences along the way. Allowing rather than stressfully striving is the key to receptivity.

The second principle, relaxation response, means that there is a relatively calm mind/body. This is in contrast to what we commonly call the fight-or-flight response. When we are being chased by a hungry tiger, we are not likely to be conscious of the fragrant jungle flowers. Physiologically, performance anxiety and striving create stress responses similar to fleeing from the tiger. If we are to really appreciate our sensations, we must first have an inner calmness.

Present-time experience is the third principle. This means that we are not caught up in our expectations of the future or in comparisons with the past. To experience stimuli, our attention must be in the present. Focusing on bodily sensations is perhaps the most powerful method to redirect our attention into present time.

This principle by no means suggests that we deny or resist our comparisons or expectations. Quite to the contrary, there are subtle bodily sensations that accompany comparisons and expectations. A sensate approach would emphasize becoming aware of and focusing our attention on these inner experiences.

The three principles of receptivity, relaxation response, and present-time experience underlie *Romantic Interludes.* To the extent that we have "lost our senses" or fail to appreciate our beautiful universe, I suggest these principles as guideposts.

• *Functions* •

How we use these principles depends on our intent. There are at least three models of how sensate approaches can function: educational, therapeutic, and transformative.

The education model views sensate processes as a means to reeducate our perception abilities. Within it we cultivate an aesthetic appreciation of our world. This model sets the tone in *Romantic Interludes.*

The therapy model, as a part of the pathology approach, mainly employs sensate processes to surface resistances, which are limiting behavioral and cognitive patterns. Underlying these patterns are unexperienced feelings/emotions, which must be experienced in order to remove the resistances.

The third function I call the transformation model. An Eastern school of thought known as tantra best presents this perspective. A Sanskrit word, tantra is often translated as "to weave" and implies the inclusive interrelatedness of phenomena. Ralph Metzner describes the historical development of tantra around the third and fourth centuries A.D. in India:

"The Upanishadic strategy of realizing the immanent self by successively stripping away the various false conceptions and perceptions of self that arise in meditation...had become distorted and perverted into practices that denied the body, rejected sense experience, and idealized penance and suffering. The tantras set up a powerful countercurrent to the ascetic tradition by affirming and glorifying the role of the body and of sense experience, and by teaching that although ordinarily they were obstacles to realization, when transformed through the esoteric practices of tantric yoga they become the very vehicles of liberation."[4]

From my study and practice in tantric traditions, I have observed that the meditation practices and rituals are principally designed to facilitate experiencing very subtle energies that constitute sensations and feelings/emotions. These energies, or "feeling-tones," are like interwoven threads that give us the cloth of experience. Since feeling-tones are very subtle, most of us are not aware of them unless we have explored meditationlike modalities.

In some ways, the tantric function also includes the educational and therapeutic models. As Metzner implies, in tantra there is definitely an appreciation of the senses. Moreover, as we refine our sensitivities and discover the deeper aspects of ourselves, we will find the heretofore unexperienced feelings/emotions.

It is not necessary to analyze the unexperienced feelings/emotions when they become experienced.

Theoretically, if a blocked feeling/emotion is fully experienced, the blocked energy flow is released. Thus, nothing would really need to be analyzed.

There is a parable to convey the tantric approach to experiencing the blocked feelings/emotions.

A person walks down the path and sees a plant in the middle of the path. Upon recognizing it as poisonous, the individual immediately turns in the opposite direction to avoid the poison.

A second person walks down the path. Upon recognizing the poisonous plant, this individual cautiously walks around the plant, acknowledging it without interacting with it—like letting a sleeping dog lie.

A third person, a tantric follower, walks down the path. Approaching the poisonous plant as an opportunity, the follower begins to consume the plant to have a direct experience. As the poison begins to take effect, the tantric, with abilities previously developed, transforms the poison into nourishing energy.

In this parable, the poison represents energy in the form of blocked feelings/emotions.

Central to the tantric perspective is the allowing of both pleasurable and unpleasurable feelings/emotions. Each provide an opportunity to experience and to manage energy.

Comparing the three approaches, the educational function emphasizes an attitude of greater appreciation of the sensory experience. The therapeutic function focuses on the problematic aspect, while the transformative function operates on the underlying energetic level.

• *Conclusion* •

I have observed that we often forget or deny our body and that this sensory unconsciousness greatly affects our sensual, sexual, and intimate expression.

Basically I have presented a sensation-focused methodology within a wellness model. While sensate approaches are by no means limited to the field of human sexuality, I suggest that enhancing our willingness and ability to experience our senses will greatly benefit sexual expression. Whether we emphasize an educational, therapeutic, or transformative function depends on our goals.

[1] Regina Sara Ryan and John W. Travis, M.D., *The Wellness Workbook* (Berkeley, CA: Ten Speed Press, 1981), p. 2.

[2] John W. Travis, M.D., "Wellness Inventory," (Wellness Resource Center, P.O. Box 5433, Mill Valley, CA 94942, 1977, 1981, 1986), Introduction page.

[3] Helen Singer Kaplan, M.D., Ph.D., *The Illustrated Manual of Sex Therapy* (New York: Quadrangle, 1975), pp. 3–4.

[4] Ralph Metzner, *Maps of Consciousness* (New York: Collier Books, 1971), pp. 30–31.

Appendix B

A Philosophy of Pleasure

The philosophy underlying *Romantic Interludes* is very simple: To have pleasure, we must be willing not to have it.

Letting go of our attachment to pleasure is the key.

∞ ∞ ∞

This is an experiential philosophy. That is, I have had experiences to which I have added a conceptual framework. This enables communication through the written and spoken word.

The words are, as a Zen Buddhist might say, like a finger pointing to the moon. Once we discover the moon, our attention no longer need remain on the finger.

• *Wu Wei and Trishna* •

Wu wei (pronounced "woo way´"), a Chinese Taoist concept, conveys the essence of being a sensuous lover: allowing things to flow in accordance with the nature of things.

The wu wei of water is to seek the lowest level. Sometimes it moves swiftly as in a stream, sometimes it remains reflectively still as in a pool, yet always available to flowing to a lower level.

To be in wu wei is not to be without direction, goals, purpose, or intention. It is neither submission nor passivity. Rather, being in wu wei means fully participating without attachment to the outcome.

The opposite of wu wei is trishna (pronounced "trish´na"), a Sanskrit word meaning grasping, clinging, or striving for an attachment.

When we see a desired object, we grasp it. Once we have it, we cling to it. Or if we do not get it, we continue striving for it. Our attention is so narrowly focused on obtaining and keeping the desired object that we forget to enjoy it. In trishna there is only limited pleasure.[1]

∞ ∞ ∞

Consider an example of wu wei and trishna while following some suggestions in *Romantic Interludes*. Suppose you have rented a hotel suite for this special

evening. You have sliced ripe fruit and have beautifully arranged it on a special platter. You've hand
whipped the whipping cream and prepared the bath
with flower petals.

But your lover does not show up.

You would probably get very angry and upset. You

might have thoughts of throwing the fruit platter against the wall, maybe count how much money and time you spent buying and preparing everything. This is trishna.

Clinging to our expectations, to our familiar methods, to our self-image of who we are or should be is trishna. When events do not turn out the way they are supposed to, our response might be boredom, fear, anger, perhaps anxiety, confusion, or physical discomfort.

On the other hand, if we were to allow events to flow in accordance with the nature of things, we might spend the evening alone enjoying the delicious fruit and whipped cream while relaxing in the warm bath. Originally we had planned all this for our lover. Now without an attachment to that outcome, we give the pleasure ritual to ourself— and thoroughly enjoy it.

If this example appears absurd, take a moment to reflect on past events when romance or sexual passion were greatly anticipated and unfulfilled.

Love, Joy, Compassion, Equanimity

In contrast to the boredom, fear, and anger of trishna, the flow of wu wei is characterized by love, joy, compassion, and equanimity.

Love is a feeling of affinity. The sensations may be a warmth or humminglike vibration in the chest near the physical heart. Nurturing is what we term the behavioral expression of our inner love feeling for another.

Love is without criteria, without value judgments of good or bad, right or wrong, beautiful or ugly. Love is available to us when we open to our common union—our communion with another.

Joy is inner celebration. Unburdened by performances and demands, we are able to give thanks.

"Com-passion" is to be "with-feeling." When we connect with another, there is a resonance of feeling qualities. The tensions of grasping prevent our perception of this resonance.

Equanimity is inner peace. Contentment rather than striving permeates our being.[2]

When we open ourselves to love, joy, compassion, and equanimity, pleasure flows naturally. In wu wei, we live fully.

• *Conclusion* •

The Zen Buddhists give us a parable about trishna and wu wei.

There were two monks walking down the path: one a novice, the other wise in the years of the monastic life. They approached a treacherous crossing of a rain-swollen stream. Standing there at the crossing was a young maiden, fearful of the torrent. Without hesitation, the older monk lifted the maiden into his arms and forded the rushing water.

Several hours later, as the two monks approached the monastery, the novice admonished the older one for breaking the established rule about not touching women.

The older monk turned and asked, "Are you still carrying the maiden?"

(This parable utilizes several prevalent images: femaleness as weak and fearful, maleness as strong, youngness as foolish, oldness as wise. Attaching such stereotypes to any individual woman, man, younger person, or older person indicates a trishna mind.)

Carrying the burdens of our attachments, we may miss the flowers along the path.

Letting go of our attachments, we become free to experience the pleasure of life.

[1] I wish to acknowledge Stan Russell for introducing me to the conceptual contrast between wu wei and trishna.

[2] My introduction to this set of concepts was through Longchenpa, a fourteenth-century Tibetan lama. See *Kindly Bent to Ease Us, Part I: Mind*, written by Longchenpa and translated by Herbert V. Guenther (Emeryville, CA: Dharma Publishing, 1975).

Appendix C

Safer-Sex,
Responsible Sex

From a wide spectrum of possible pleasure activities, *Romantic Interludes* emphasizes the sensual and intimate qualities. Many of the adventures described can be followed with little or no concern about transmission of the Human Immunodeficiency Virus (HIV), more commonly known as the AIDS virus.

Without attempting to be a complete safer-sex manual, this appendix will briefly examine some guidelines and risk-reduction methods for activities in this book. Here *safer-sex* refers to forms of sensual or sexual play that either reduce or eliminate possibilities of HIV transmission.

Please remember that while research has greatly increased our knowledge of the nature of HIV transmission, further research could lead us to conclude that some of the following safer-sex methods are overly cautious while others are insufficiently restrictive.

• *Casual Contact* •

Basically, HIV is rather fragile and difficult to transmit.

Repeatedly, research studies have shown that the virus is not transmitted through casual contact. Household members sharing in nonsexual daily activities with people with AIDS have *not* become infected. To the contrary, it is the person with AIDS who faces risk when the HIV infection has become very severe. Then other household members could be the source of exposure to microorganisms that could cause illness in an impaired immune system.

• *Bidirectional Transmission* •

AIDS can in no way be considered a "their" disease. The virus has no regard for sexual orientation or gender: Male-to-female, female-to-male, male-to-male, and female-to-female transmissions are all proven to occur.

• *Transmission Mediums* •

Public health and medical sources repeatedly advise that infected *blood, ejaculate, rectal secretions,* and *vaginal/cervical secretions* are the principal transmission mediums.

HIV has also been located in other bodily fluids. While there seems to be no concern about transmission via tears and sweat, some researchers have more reservation than others regarding the safeness of saliva and urine.

It should be stressed that having contact with bodily fluids is of concern only when both of two conditions exist. First, the bodily fluid is from an HIV-infected person. Second, the infected person's bodily fluid enters another's system. Since we may not know with certainty our own or another's health status at this minute, we may choose either to refrain from an activity or to participate in a way that minimizes transmission possibilities.

• *Protection Methods* •

Physical-barrier protection is the most frequently recommended form of safer-sex protection. Depending on the nature of the activity, the most common forms of physical-barrier protection are latex condoms, latex or vinyl (plastic) medical examination gloves, plastic wrap, and latex dental dams. (The gloves are now common in pharmacies, and dental dams often are available from medical or dental supply companies.)

Latex condoms are increasingly popular. Unfortunately, it is not commonly known that vegetable oils and petroleum-based products deteriorate latex. Even more unfortunate, some sensual/sexual accessory oils and lotions do not clearly indicate they contain such ingredients. Use only water-based lubricants with latex condoms.

Plastic condoms are quickly entering the market, and some people find them more sensuous. These condoms *can* be used with oil.

Regarding natural, lamb-skin condoms, researchers are recommending *not* to use these condoms because they are sometimes too porous and allow the AIDS virus to pass through.

The latex or vinyl gloves are for use when there is hand contact with bodily fluids. While the cautions about vegetable oil and petroleum-based products apply to latex gloves as well, there seems to be no similar concern with vinyl gloves.

Latex dental dams and household plastic wrap function as protection during oral contact.

In addition to physical barriers, there are chemical barriers. Nonoxynol-9, a commonly used ingredient in spermicides, in sufficient concentrations can kill HIV as well as some other pathogens upon contact. Some people, however, are allergic to products containing nonoxynol-9. Changing brands might solve this problem.

Chemical barriers can be used in addition to the physical barriers if you wish to have increased risk reduction—occasionally, a condom will break or slip off.

Supplementally, any detergent or cleaning solution containing nonoxynol-9 can provide a hygienic cleaning of vibrators and other shared sexual accessories.

• *Romantic Interludes* •

"Yuk," you may be thinking by now. "I'd rather give up sex than follow all this clinical stuff!" This is exactly what many others thought when they began to hear about AIDS and safer-sex.

Abstinence from sex is a viable and valuable option. But abstinence elected out of despair and suppression, some sex therapists are finding, may lead, like dieting, to uncontrollable, indiscriminate binges. Fortunately, there are other options.

Should we choose sexual abstinence, it is important to remember, as Ashley Montagu documents in *Touching*, that touch is a basic human need. Without touch, we wither away and die, emotionally if not physically. Sexual procreation, on the other hand, is a basic need for continuation of the species, not for the continuation of the individual.[1] Many of the techniques in *Romantic Interludes*, such as foot bathing, facial massage, and unison breathing, can be very nurturing, nonsexual activities.

Always, there are options.

Sexual expression, happily, does not have to be defined solely as pelvic-pelvic or oral-pelvic contact. In fact, one of the original intentions in writing *Romantic Interludes* was to encourage broadening the reader's horizons beyond the standard entrée of intercourse. Inadvertently, then, most of the techniques are considered "no risk" or "very low risk" activities. This is the case *only* if the skin is in healthy condition and without any cuts or cracks.

The major exception would be Chapter 23, *The Three-Hands Massage*. Following safer-sex guidelines here would definitely mean using a condom and not allowing massage oil on a latex condom if the oil is vegetable based or contains petroleum products.

For the oral activities of Chapters 8, 9, and 10, you could refrain from the anal and genital areas, especially if the recipient is menstruating. To be on the extremely cautious side, you might refrain from kisses that exchange saliva. Perhaps explore using a dental dam or plastic wrap.

For the genital massage and pelvic bathing in

Chapters 11 through 18 and Chapter 20, you could use vinyl gloves. While condoms could be used with the strokes on the penis, most of these specific strokes will probably be more pleasurable when using the gloves instead.

Another alternative is to be sexually exclusive with one person after both partners have tested negative on the HIV antibody test. (A "negative" means HIV was not found in the blood.) This approach, of course, requires honesty on the part of both partners.

In one sense, these suggestions may be overly simplistic, since lovemaking is often more extensive than the specific exercises in this book.[2] But in most cases, exploring the suggested adventures and taking precautions whenever you feel at risk can bring many moments of love and romance.[3]

• *Responsible Sex* •

Before becoming lost in a maze of safer-sex dos and don'ts, let's step back and look at a larger context—a perspective I call *responsible sex.*

First, each of us can make choices about our comfort zone: what we are willing and unwilling to do sensually, sexually, and intimately, and with whom. Always, there are options, and sex need not simply equal pelvis-pelvis penetration.

Second, we can take responsibility for our own health. This means becoming informed about sexual health and following methods that maintain our health. This also means that we may have to choose behaviors based on the possibility of a sexual partner not communicating honestly about his or her sexual activities with others.

Third, we can be willing to communicate with our partner. When our wants and needs differ, we can negotiate to find a mutual comfort zone. Without being blindly rigid, we can explore avenues.

AIDS and other communicable conditions do not mean the end of sex. Greater honesty and sensual creativity are boons to lovemaking. Following these principles enriches more than our sexual life. Relationships and our general well-being are also deeply nurtured.

These principles are keys. We need only choose to use them.

[1] Ashley Montagu, *Touching: The Human Significance of the Skin* (New York: Harper & Row, 1971).

[2] There are many safer-sex books now available, such as *The Complete Guide to Safer Sex*, edited by Ted McIlvenna (Ft. Lee, NJ: Barricade Books, 1992).

[3] I would like to express my appreciation to Clark Taylor, Ph.D., for his consultations on the more recent safer-sex research.

About the Author, Collaborator, and Illustrator

The Author

After leaving academia, Kenneth Ray Stubbs, Ph.D., moved to the San Francisco Bay Area. There he became a certified masseur, a certified sexologist, and studied a wide range of Western and Eastern approaches to health and sexuality.

Finding touch to be an effective means for creating intimacy, Ray began to teach courses in sensuality and sexuality for couples. This led to a faculty position at the Institute for Advanced Study of Human Sexuality, where he designed a training program in Sensate Therapy.

Currently, Dr. Stubbs devotes his time fully to

writing and has written several books on sexuality and spirituality.

The Collaborator

Louise-Andrée Saulnier, Ph.D(c)., has been in private practice as a sex therapist in Quebec City since 1989. After receiving her training as a sexologist at the Institute for the Advanced Study of Human Sexuality in San Francisco, for two years she hosted her own daily television show on sexuality.

Ms. Saulnier frequently lectures to medical professionals and the general public, and has served as a principal consultant on the French edition of an human sexuality encyclopedia. Her writings have appeared in professional journals and books as well as lay publications.

The Illustrator

Kyle Spencer is a freelance illustrator residing in Oakland, California. She has a bachelor's degree from the Academy of Art College in San Francisco. Her art also appears in *Erotic Massage, Secret Sexual Positions* and *The Clitoral Kiss* as well as *Tantra: The Magazine* and *Ecstasy Journal*.

Acknowledgments

Louise-Andrée Saulnier is the major source of inspiration for my writing *Romantic Interludes*. Her love and her erotic responsiveness influenced many of the chapters. She is also the translator for the French edition. It is only fitting that she be acknowledged as collaborator of the American edition.

Kyle Spencer's illustrations have such a soft sensuality, adding a communication that beautifully conveys the underlying messages I attempt with the written word. I am deeply grateful for her abilities and support.

Many others have contributed to this book. Martin Speich was the editor who first invited me to write the monthly column that evolved into this book. They as well as Yvon Dallaire and Doris Grünhut provided spaces in Quebec City and Zurich for me to write.

Direct financial support for this project has come

from Al Ruiz, Anne Wiewel, Carolyn Hardies, Christian Zangerle, John Jaeger, Louise-Andrée Saulnier, Mary Campisi, Paul Johnson, and Yvon Dallaire.

The various pleasuring techniques have been suggested by or discovered with these sensuous people: Adrian Patterson, Anne Hooper, Beverly Whipple, Betty Dodson, Joan Kerr, Joani Blank, Joe Kramer, Joseph Gutstadt, Lynn Craig, Mary Jane Harper, Mary Vinette, Nora LaCorte, Stan Russell, Sun Dancer, and others.

The quotes and anecdotes come from Andrew Reekie, Emily Williams, Hunter Morey, Jeanie Aspen, Lauri Jeffries, Lorene Allen, Lori Van Humbeck, Marguerite Wingrove, Rampujan, Tom Irons, and Veronica Friedman, amongst others.

Special thanks also go to Chyrelle D. Chasen, Sandy Trupp, Richard Stodart, Bert Cutler, Karen Kummerfeldt, Mary Chapman-McIntosh, Spring Gibson, Dorothy Kelly, Al Freedman, and the Marin Small Publishers Association. Dr. Clark Taylor's and Molly Hogan's safer-sex suggestions have proved invaluable for this edition.

∞ ∞ ∞

Most of all, I thank my mother and grandmother for those many years of putting me to sleep by scratching my back. That taught me the essence of touch and nurturing.